GOLF SKILLS

GOLF SKILLS
THE PLAYER'S GUIDE

In memory of Payne Stewart,
the perfect gentleman

ROGER HYDER

Grange
BOOKS

A QUANTUM BOOK

Produced by
Quantum Publishing Ltd
6 Blundell Street
London N7 9BH

This edition printed 2008

Published by Grange Books
an imprint of Grange Books Ltd.
35, Riverside
Sir Thomas Longley Road
Medway City Estate, Rochester
Kent ME2 4DP
www.grangebooks.co.uk

ISBN: 978-1-84804-018-2

QUMGLFS

Manufactured in Hong Kong by
Regent Publishing Services Ltd
Printed in Singapore by
Star Standard Industries (Pte) Ltd

Special thanks to Deni Booker and Danny French and Chart Hills Golf Club

INTRODUCTION

The story I hear time and time again from the players I teach is that golf instruction books treat you either as an outright beginner who has never played golf before or, conversely, as a tournament professional with a near-perfect swing who requires a complicated set of drills. I have assumed that you have already started to play golf, have a problem with your game, and are looking for advice to correct it.

The first part of *Golf Skills* looks in detail at the different types of poor shots and their most common causes. For every cause of a swing fault you will find a detailed remedy, and in many cases a helpful tip.

The second section of the book takes you out on the course and contains tips and drills from highly respected professionals to help you with different aspects of your game – the long game, the short game, and putting, for example.

As with most golf instruction books, I have written this book with a right-handed golfer in mind. All you lefties reading this book obviously have to exchange the word left for right, and right for left where appropriate.

Golf can be a difficult and at times frustrating game and it is my hope that *Golf Skills* will help you with your chosen sport. In fact if you work hard on your swing by following the drills and exercises in this book I know your game will improve. Golf is a wonderful sport and for myself and many like me it is a wonderful vocation, but remember, golf is just a game and as the great Walter Hagen once said 'Remember to take the time to smell the roses along the way'. I hope you enjoy reading the book as much as I have writing it. **Roger Hyder**

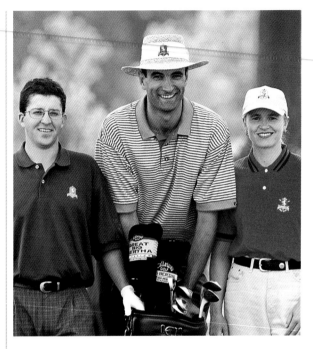

Danny French, left, is the Head Professional and Director of Instruction at Chart Hills Golf Club. He is an accomplished player and one of the most respected professionals in the South of England.

Roger Hyder has been a professional golfer for nearly 20 years. He is a fully qualified PGA Professional and is Director of Golf and General Manager at Chart Hills Golf Club in Kent.

Deni Booker, right, represents the Nick Faldo-designed Chart Hills Golf Club on the Ladies European Tour. Since qualifying for the European Tour in 1995 she has had considerable success both in Europe and in her native Australia. Deni is a previous winner of the Italian Open.

GOLFING TERMS

ADDRESS The positioning of the club and body prior to playing a stroke.

APPROACH SHOT A shot made from close proximity onto the green.

BORROW When putting, the amount of compensation allowed for slopes, wind etc. Also referred to as break.

CARRY The distance the ball travels through the air.

CASTING THE CLUB Premature uncocking or unhinging of the wrists in the downswing.

CHIP A short low-flying shot, normally to a green, where the ball rolls more than it carries.

CUT A shot where clockwise spin is imparted on the ball and which produces a left-to-right shot pattern.

DRAW For right-handed players, a shot that moves slightly right to left in flight.

EXPLOSION SHOT or **SPLASH SHOT** A shot played from a good lie in the bunker and created by the clubface 'splashing' into the sand and removing the ball on a bed of sand.

FADE For right-handed players, a shot that moves slightly left to right in flight.

FAT SHOT A shot where the club head makes contact with the ground before the ball. Also called chunking.

FLAT SWING A swing that has a path more around the body than upright.

FLUFFING or **CHUNKING** A *fat shot* when chipping or pitching.

HARDPAN Hard, worn and bare ground.

HITTING FROM THE TOP see *casting*.

HOODED CLUBFACE Delofting and slight closing of the clubface, either at address or during the swing.

HOOK An exaggerated draw, a shot that moves in flight considerably from right to left.

HOSEL The part of the club that connects the clubhead and the shaft.

LAID OFF Position of the club where the backswing is too flat and the club at the top of the backswing is aiming to the left of the target.

LIE Position of the ball after it has come to rest.

LOB A short high shot that lands softly with little roll.

LOFT The angle of the clubface in relation to the ground and the vertical. The more horizontal the clubface, the greater the loft.

PLUGGED BALL A ball lying in its own pitch mark.

PULL HOOK For right-handed players, a shot that starts left of target and curves even further left during flight.

PULL SHOT For right-handed players, a shot that flies straight left of target.

RELEASE The movement created by the body and club that allows the clubface to return to square and accompanying freeing of the stored power created in the backswing,

REVERSE PIVOT The incorrect movement of the upper body towards the target on the backswing,

SHANK Striking the ball with the heel (hosel) of the club causing the ball to fly very high but only a short distance.

SHAPING THE BALL Encouraging the ball to move in flight either left to right (a fade) or right to left (a draw).

SKYING Hitting the ball with the top half of the club and causing the ball to fly very high and travel a short distance.

SLICE For right-handed players, a ball that flies exaggeratedly from left to right.

SMOTHERED SHOT A shot hit with an excessively closed clubface causing the ball to fail to take off.

SQUARING THE CLUBFACE UP Movement by the body to return the clubface on the downswing so that it is at right angles to the ball-to-target line at impact.

STANCE The positioning of the feet when addressing the ball.

SWINGPATH The direction the club is swung in relation to the ball-to-target line. An in-to-out swingpath is when the clubhead travels from inside the ball-to-target line (nearer to the body) to outside the ball-to-target line (away from the body). An out-to-in swingpath is the opposite.

TAKEAWAY The club's initial movement away from the ball.

THIN SHOT A low-flying mis-hit or swing fault where the club catches the ball on the equator and slightly on the up.

TOPPED SHOT A shot that fails to get off the ground. This is caused by striking the ball above its equator.

YIPS An involuntary loss of control over the hands and arms when putting.

Faults, Diagnoses and Remedies

- Pulls and Slices
- Pushes and Hooks
- Mis-hits
- Short Game and Putting Problems

CHAPTER ONE
Pulls and Slices

The pull shot is a shot that flies straight left of target and is very closely related to the slice. The sliced shot is one that normally starts slightly left of target and then veers out to the right. The main difference between the two is that the pull is more prevalent with the short irons and the slice is more common with the long irons and woods (due to the lack of loft on the longer clubs).

In both cases, the club approaches the ball on an out-to-in swingpath but with the clubface facing left of target for a pull shot and facing right of target for a sliced shot.

I approach the faults in this chapter in the order in which you would prepare to take your shot, running from aim to downswing and finishing with the less common faults that you may find causing your pulls and slices.

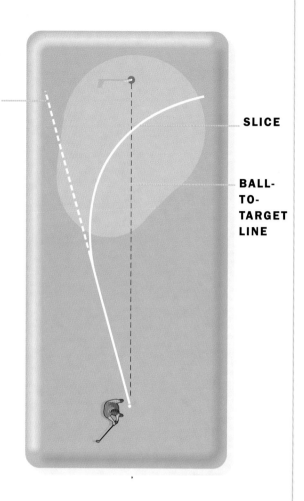

PULL

SLICE

BALL-TO-TARGET LINE

AIM

Quite simply, aim is the direction in which the clubhead faces at set up, and (assuming a consistent swingpath is achieved), is invariably where the ball will finish. The difference between the pull and the slice is that, just before you hit the ball, the clubface will be pointing left of target for a pull and right of target for a slice.

✔ CORRECTING YOUR AIM

Top amateurs and professionals alike place a great deal of emphasis on the "ball-to-target-line," the imaginary line running from the ball to target. For a well-aimed shot, the leading edge of the clubface should always be at a right angle to the ball-to-target line.

A popular pre-shot routine advocated by such golfing greats as Jack Nicklaus and Greg Norman is to stand several feet behind the ball, as if lining up a putt, and try to pick out a divot or a similar mark on the ground approximately 4 to 5 feet (1 to 1.5 m) in front of the ball and on the ball-to-target line. Then, focus on this mark when setting up, rather than trying to line up on the target somewhere off in the distance. The point about lining up on a mark only a short distance in front of the ball is that both ball and mark are in your field of view at the same time.

GRIP

❌ Pull grip

For a "pull shot," one or both hands will invariably be too "strong", that is, located too far underneath the handle when viewed from the address position.

❌ Slicer's grip

A slicer's hold on the club will be invariably be "weak," or too far on top of the handle with the line formed between thumb and forefinger pointing to the left of the chin.

❌ "Palmed" grip

Another factor common to most slicers is that the grip is too much in the palm of the left hand. This prevents the wrists from cocking and uncocking correctly during the swing, and makes it difficult to square up the clubface at impact. If you need proof of a "palmed" grip, check your golf glove for wear. If you have a tendency to wear a hole in the glove on the heel of your hand, then you have a palmed grip.

▶ Try to hold the club in a more neutral position. As you look down at your grip from the address position you should be able to see 2 or 3 knuckles of the left hand, no more and no less.

▶ Looking at your left hand, the line formed between the left thumb and forefinger should point to an area halfway between your right shoulder and chin.

▶ The club's handle should run from a point just above the base of the little finger of your left hand, across the fingers to the middle joint of the forefinger.

TIP

Don't let the term "grip" make you feel that you must hold the club as if strangling it. The pressure of your grip should be firm and sure but not overly tight.

The right hand should be placed on the handle in such a way that the line formed between thumb and forefinger once again points to a position between the chin and right shoulder.

GRIP VARIATIONS

✔ Vardon
Depending on the size of your hands and your strength, the little finger of the right hand can fit in the groove between the forefinger and middle finger of the left hand (the Vardon grip).

✔ Interlock
Alternatively, it can interlock with the forefinger of the left hand (advisable for people with small hands or thick short fingers).

✔ Baseball
Finally, players with weaker hands and senior golfers might try using this baseball two-handed grip.

BALL POSITION

✗ Ball Forward in Stance

Another factor common to pullers and slicers is ball position. Invariably, the ball is placed too far forward (that is, toward the target) in the stance.

✗ Open Shoulder

This ball position forces the line across your shoulders to point left of target at address. This in turn will encourage you to swing on an out-to-in swingpath.

✓ Correct

By simply pushing the ball back in the stance a little you can achieve a much more comfortable set-up.

Low Handicap Player

I like to see more experienced players play with the ball opposite the left heel for a wood shot, and moving back gradually to a position just short of midway between the feet for a short iron.

High Handicap Player

Less experienced players should have the ball positioned for a wood 1 in (2.5 cm) inside the left heel, and for short irons, back to midway between the feet.

STANCE

Most slicers have a tendency to stand to the ball with their feet too far apart. This restricts the natural movement of the body through the swing and encourages what is known as a reverse pivot.

❌ The reverse pivot is the failure to shift one's weight onto the right leg on the backswing, and onto the left leg on the follow-through.

❌ The weight remains on the left leg during the backswing, forcing the hips to twist to the right.

❌ The weight shifts onto the right leg on the follow-through, pivoting the right hip forward.

TIP

Sometimes, after correcting the width of your stance, your left knee can shoot out towards the ball, which will encourage you to reverse pivot. If you find this, try to keep your left knee still throughout the backswing. This may be a little difficult at first because your back and trunk will start to stretch properly. In fact it is this stretching that builds up the power in your stroke and gives you distance on your shots.

 ## CORRECTING YOUR STANCE

The width of the stance varies according to the height and build of the golfer. For all players, as the club length shortens, the width of the stance should narrow slightly.

 ### Tall & Athletic

A tall player with an athletic swing should stand, for a medium to long shot, with the inside of his heels shoulder-width apart.

 ### Short or Less Flexible

The shorter or less flexible golfer should stand, once again for medium to long shots, with the outside of his heels shoulder-width apart.

BODY ALIGNMENT

✗ Every slicer, and most golfers who pull the ball left, have the line through their shoulders or hips or feet aiming left of target. All or any of these misaligned can cause you to swing across the line and thus off target.

✓ CORRECTING ALIGNMENT
The line drawn through the feet, hips, and shoulders should be parallel to the ball-to-target line. While playing on the course, a simple adjustment check is to hold a club parallel to the ground across the middle of your thighs. This will give you a good indication of where your feet and hips are pointing.

> **TIP**
> When practicing on the range, place a club on the ground near the ball and parallel to the ball-to-target line. Then place another club on the ground across the front of your feet. This club should also be parallel to the ball-to-target line and *not* pointing directly at the target. Then start hitting shots while making sure that your hips and shoulders are parallel to your feet.

POSTURE

 Unless a golfer has good set angles at address, he will find it very difficult to swing the club on a consistent plane. Very few amateurs have good posture. Stand on a first tee anywhere in the world and watch how golfers stoop, crouch, stretch, and bend at address.

✓ CORRECTING POSTURE

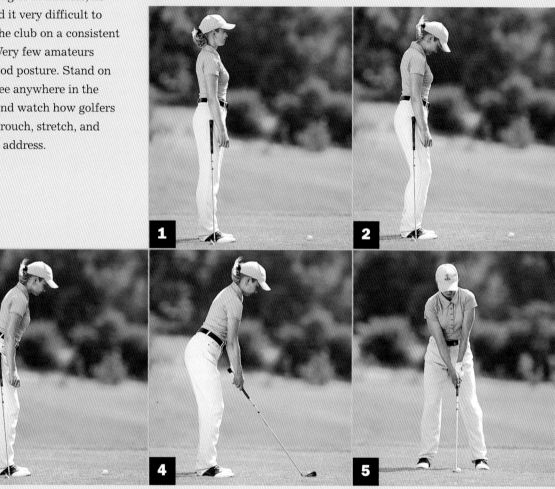

1 Stand up straight with arms at your side.

2 Look down at your shoelaces. Now bend your knees until you can no longer see the shoelaces.

3 Keeping your back straight, push your bottom out, and move your head out toward the ball, keeping your chin up off your chest.

4 and 5 Let your arms hang straight down and grip the club. Tilt your left shoulder (or your right, if left-handed) up a little and check that your body weight is on the balls of your feet.

BACKSWING

 At the start of this chapter, I said that with pulls and slices the clubhead approaches the ball on an out-to-in swingpath, but with the clubface aiming left of target for a pull shot, and aiming right of target for a sliced shot.

A common cause of an out-to-in swingpath is the tendency to "pick the club up" at the start of the backswing. In other words, the backswing is incorrectly initiated by the clubhead and hands with very little movement from the body. Therefore, the clubhead goes outside the ball-to-target line. Depending on whether the clubface has been rolled open or not, a pull or slice will result.

✔ CORRECTING YOUR BACKSWING

The start of the backswing (or move away) should be initiated by the clubhead, hands, shoulders and navel all moving away from the ball together. This will ensure that you swing the club back on plane.

▶ DRILL

This simple little drill can be used anywhere, be it on the course, on the range, or even at home watching TV.

1 Place a club on the ground running from behind your left heel to your right toe. Then address an imaginary ball with another club. Next, slide the club up inside your grip until the butt of the club is sticking against your navel.

2 Now turn everything (clubhead, hands, shoulders, and navel) away in one piece.

3

3 You will know you have got the move right by checking that, at the maximum point of this one-movement backswing, the club you are holding is parallel to the club between your feet.

DOWNSWING

I am sure many of you will have heard of the expression "hitting from the top." The situation most commonly arises when medium to high handicappers are trying to hit the ball too hard. Instead of a nice rhythmic transition from the top of the backswing into the downswing, led by the uncoiling of the hips and legs, a violent heave by the upper body occurs that throws the right shoulder, and inevitably the clubhead, out of plane.

✔ CORRECTING DOWNSWING

The correct downswing is initiated by the legs and hips – or, more specifically, by the left knee. When the lower body launches the downswing it does two things:

- It shallows out the swingpath and ensures that the clubhead is attacking the ball on an in-to-out swingpath.
- It progressively and smoothly unleashes the natural power that we associate with the great players.

▶ DRILL

Stand with your feet just inches (several centimeters) apart at the address position, keeping your forearms "soft." Using a 6-iron, make a full swing, and try to hit the ball as short a distance as you can but in the air. Notice how your lower body initiates the downswing and your hands release at impact. As you get the hang of this, try to raise the tempo of your swing slightly and hit the ball farther, but do make sure that your forearms remain soft and relaxed at address.

OTHER REASONS
FOR PULLS AND SLICES

GRIP

Slicers often grip the club too tightly, preventing the club from releasing at impact. When holding the club, light pressure should be felt only in the last three fingers of the left hand, and the middle two fingers of the right.

▼ PRO-WATCHING ▼

Severiano Ballesteros had a great mental image to help him with his grip. He would imagine that he was holding a small bird in his hands. Grip too tightly and he would squash the bird; too loosely and the bird would escape from his hand.

DOWNSWING

How many times have you heard one golfer trying to help another with the lines: "Keep your head still!" or "Keep your head down!" Let me clear this up once and for all. The only place to keep your head down or still is on the putting green.

X Keeping your head still will make your shoulders tilt rather than turn on the backswing. This, and the lack of shift in weight also caused by a still head, is another cause of a reverse pivot. The only way to get the club back to the ball is to keep the weight on the right side on the downswing, causing an inevitable pull or slice.

✓ CORRECTING DOWNSWING
To overcome this, turn your head slightly at address so that your left eye is looking at the back of the ball. Also, allow your head to rotate a little more as you turn your body away from the target during the backswing.

✖ KEEPING YOUR HEAD DOWN

The other part of the problem is "keeping your head down." The player who heeds this well-meaning advice may find that he stops skulling or topping the ball for a while; but as it is not the reason for skulling or topping, the problem will soon return, only with an addition – a slice.

The reason for this is that usually a "head downer" has his chin almost pinned to his chest. This stops the shoulders from turning fully on the backswing. Then the only way to get the club up to the top of the swing is for the arms to "separate" from the turning motion of the trunk, and ride up the chest. The golfer will now have the club on a plane that is far too upright.

The downswing now starts from outside the intended swingpath. Because the head is still stuck to the chest on the downswing, the right shoulder cannot swing freely through the shot, and the arms and club finish in a very short follow-through that remains very much outside the desired swingpath. You have now completed a very successful out-to-in swing – the perfect recipe for a slice!

  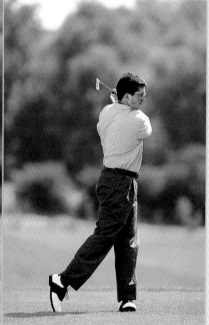

✔ CORRECTING HEAD POSITION

To overcome this problem, lift your chin clear of your chest at address. Try to develop the feeling that you are looking down your nose at the ball. Then, simply keep your eye on the ball throughout the backswing and follow-through. This includes the ball rising off the ground following impact. By doing this you are allowing the chin to be "knocked out of the way" by the right shoulder on the follow-through, which creates a high, flowing finish to the swing and ensures that you watch the ball throughout the strike.

STANCE

✗ Many slicers stand too close to the ball at the address position. This encourages the golfer to pick the club up too steeply and become cramped at the top of the backswing. As a consequence, the only way to attack the ball is to throw the club out of the swingpath from the top and bring the club down on an out-to-in swingpath.

✓ CORRECTING STANCE
When taking the normal address position, ensure the following is achieved:

1 You should be comfortably bent over from the hips with your rear end sticking out.
2 Your knees should be slightly flexed and your arms hanging down relaxed. Now, when addressing the ball, the butt end of the club should be 4–5 in (10–12 cm) from your inner left thigh.

BACKSWING

❌ Often a player who is consciously trying to avoid swinging out-to-in (and thus slicing) will turn the clubface inside the ball-to-target line on the backswing so that the clubhead is "inside "his hands on the ball-to-target line – that is, too far around the right side of his body. Although the clubface should move back inside the ball-to-target line, if you exaggerate this movement it will cramp you at the midpoint of your backswing. Then the only way you can complete the backswing is to lift the club up steeply. This in turn forces your swing out of plane and encourages you to swing from out-to-in on the downswing.

✔ CORRECTING BACKSWING

To avoid doing this, try to develop the feeling that the butt end of the club initiates the backswing. Also, try to imagine that you are brushing your right thigh with the butt. Both of these thoughts will encourage you to swing the club inside the ball-to-target line while keeping the clubhead "outside" your hands.

CHAPTER TWO
Pushes and Hooks

Just as the pull and slice shots are related, so too are the push and hook shots. Both are usually problems of a low-handicap player. The push shot is one that flies straight out to the right of target for a right-handed player. The hook shot starts slightly right of target, and then turns and finishes left of the target. The hook is more common with woods and long irons; the push is more prevalent with short irons. In both cases, the club is swung on an in-to-out swingpath (see page 43), the difference between the two shots being that the clubface is square to the swingpath for a push, and closed to the swingpath for a hook.

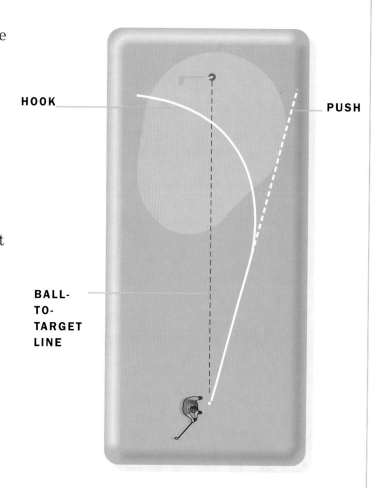

HOOK

PUSH

BALL-TO-TARGET LINE

AIM

One of the first things to look for when hooking or pushing the ball is to check the clubface aim at address. Normally the clubface is not a factor when pushing the ball, but when a right-handed golfer hooks a shot, the aim of the clubface will have been aiming left of the target at impact.

TIP

When on the practice ground or driving range, place a clubshaft running from the ball toward the target. This will make squaring up the clubface a lot easier.

✓ **CORRECTING AIM**
Take your normal stance, check your posture, and place the clubhead immediately behind the ball. Try to ensure that the front edge of the clubhead is at a right angle to the ball-to-target line.

▶ To make sure you have correct aim, grip the club and then hold it out in front of you at waist height, parallel to the ground. If the clubface is square to the target, the leading edge of the clubhead will be pointing straight up at the sky.

GRIP

The grip rarely causes pushed shots but it is probably the most common factor responsible for the hook shot. One or both hands will be in too "strong" a position – that is, placed too far underneath around the handle as you look down on it at address.

This, in effect, closes the clubface at impact and therefore puts hookspin on the ball. As you look down at your grip, you will notice that the line formed between the thumb and forefinger on one or both of your hands will be pointing up straight at your right shoulder or even to the right of that!

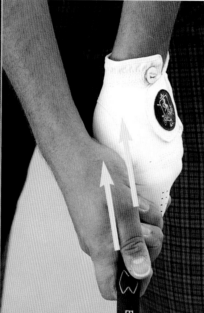

✗ Hooker's Grip
The lines formed between the thumbs and forefingers are at a shallow angle to the club handle.

✗ Neutral Grip
The lines between the thumbs and forefingers are nearer the vertical.

✓ CORRECTING GRIP
As with my advice for remedying a slicer's grip (see page 13), try to place both hands more on top of the shaft, so that the line formed between thumb and forefinger on each hand is pointing to a spot midway between your chin and right shoulder.

BALL POSITION

Incorrect positioning of the ball in the stance is, for most players, the single biggest reason for hitting push shots and is also a major contributing factor in hitting hook shots. Although the problem is common among better players it can also affect high handicap players as well.

1 If the ball is positioned too far back in the stance (too near the back foot) the left shoulder is pulled forward and the shoulders "close", that is, point right of the ball-to-target line.

2 As the shoulders close, the resulting swing is too much inside-to-out. This causes either a push or a hook depending on where the clubface is facing at impact.

✓ CORRECTING BALL POSITION

I am often asked where an average player should place the ball. The answer is *just before* the bottom of the swing for iron shots and *at* the bottom of the swing for wood shots (or even slightly forward for tee shots). The reason for this is twofold: the longer shafts of wooden clubs dictate that the ball is farther away from you; and a sweeping motion is the desired action for wood shots, while a descending blow is needed for iron shots and therefore needs to be closer. Better players should have the back of the ball opposite their left heel for a wood shot and move back gradually to a position just short of midway for a short-iron shot. The average handicapper should have the ball about 1 in (2 cm) inside the left heel, moving back gradually to midway between the feet for short irons.

STANCE

✗ A hook shot is rarely attributable to a poor stance, but stance may be a reason for pushing. Slightly more common among better players, the cause of this is just like that of a slicer with a too wide stance.

The difference between the two faults (slicing and pushing the ball) is that the slicer does not get his weight back onto the right side on the backswing, and therefore reverse pivots (see page 18) The golfer who pushes the ball has no such problem on the backswing, but he fails to transfer his weight through to the left side on the downswing, so that the hands have to take over. This fault is nearly always coupled with the ball being set too far back (too close) in the stance at address. In fact, much like the chicken and the egg, a poor stance can cause poor ball position, and poor ball position can cause poor stance.

✓ CORRECTING STANCE

The stances of the slicer and pusher are very similar as are the remedies. For a wood shot, the heels should be no more than shoulder-width apart.

The stance should narrow for shorter clubs because the swing also shortens and the legs and hips have less time to clear. A narrower stance also allows the legs to move more quickly.

BODY ALIGNMENT

X The question of body alignment proves that in golf two wrongs never make a right. The majority of better players hit the ball with draw spin, so that the ball moves slightly from right to left in the air. While it is useful to shape the ball (as all top professionals do), under pressure the draw may become a violent hook, a most destructive shot. Lee Trevino used to say,

"You can talk to a fade, but a hook won't listen!"

If shots persistently veer to the left, even good players (who should know better) may align the body to the right of target to compensate. Under pressure, or when a player's timing is wrong, this will only exaggerate the fault, and the draw or push will become a consistent hook.

✓ CORRECTING BODY ALIGNMENT
Your body should always be square to the target. Imaginary lines drawn across your feet, hips, and shoulders should be parallel to the ball-to-target line. This will ensure that you do not have to overcompensate for a misaligned shot with a violent hooking action.

POSTURE

✕ PROBLEMS WITH POSTURE

The two main faults with posture at address are the distribution of your body weight on your feet and the relative height of your shoulders.

If your weight is too much on your heels, you will notice two things:

• Your hook shots are actually pull hooks. That is, they start left of target and then hook even farther left.

• On completing your swing your feet will have moved away from your original body line. Invariably you will have taken the club back too far inside the bodyline on the backswing or "pulled" the body away from the ball at impact.

If your right shoulder is too low at address your head will almost certainly be too far back in the set up and it will also force the shoulders to close in relation to the ball-to-target line. This in turn makes it very difficult to swing the club back on the ball-to-target line.

✓ CORRECTING POSTURE

At address try to place your body weight in such a way that you feel that it is over the balls of your feet. Alternatively, if it is clear that your problem is not with distribution of your body weight, then it will be with the position of your right shoulder which will have dropped too low. Try to raise your right shoulder and right elbow at address so that they are only *just below* their counterparts on the left side of your body. A full-length mirror will help you make the necessary adjustment.

Make sure you keep your shoulders and elbows parallel.

1 With just your right hand on the club, place the clubhead behind the ball, while at the same time placing your right foot at a point directly opposite the back of the ball.

2 Then place your left hand on the club and at the same time move your left foot into position.

3 Now check the width of your stance and your ball position. At first you will feel that your body is aiming left of target and that your right shoulder is above the left, but persevere and you will soon start to reap the benefits.

BACKSWING

✕ A common fault among those with more athletic swings is an exaggerated rolling of the clubface inside the ball-to-target line at the start of the backswing. This creates a very flat turn, with the clubshaft at the top of the backswing pointing right of the target. This will force an exaggerated in-to-out swingpath on the downswing with the result being a push or hook.

✓ CORRECTING BACKSWING

Because the fault is caused by the hands and arms working independently of the body, you need to develop a correct takeaway from the ball in which the club, hands, arms, and torso all move as a unit.

Try practicing with another ball positioned approximately 18 in (45 cm) behind the one you intend to hit and about 1 in (2.5 cm) inside the ball-to-target line. The intention is to hit the target ball but not before you have swept the second ball away on the backswing.

This drill will not only encourage a correct takeaway, but will also improve your tempo.

The right-shoulder fault is caused by a poor set-up routine. I like the routine used by Greg Norman and Seve Ballesteros. Seve Ballesteros's set up proves that the best don't forget the fundamental basics of the set up and that trusted routines really do work.

DOWNSWING

1

2

❌ Often in the downswing a player can be cramped while returning the clubface to the ball, causing him to either block the shot to the right or panic at the last moment, over-compensate with the hands, and thus hook the ball. This is predominately a fault of a good player and usually stems from two particular swing thoughts.

1 The first results from overpulling the club down with the left hand on the downswing, and trying too hard to swing in-to-out.

2 The second is an exaggeration of legendary golf champion Ben Hogan's tip of starting the downswing with an accentuated turn of the hips.

With both faults, the right elbow is bent too far coming into impact and the angle of the clubshaft is far too steep.

At the top of the backswing the whole body should feel coiled or wound up, with the shoulders having turned 90° and the hips 40°. The start of the downswing (otherwise known as the transition) should commence with the left shoulder and left hip rotating back to the address position and the body weight transferring from right side to left side. If a player concentrates solely on turning his hips back to the ball, the right shoulder will tend to dip and the club will become jammed behind the right hip.

✓ CORRECTING YOUR DOWNSWING

If you think your problem stems from the first of these swing faults, try to hit shots off a tee using only your right arm. This will encourage you to straighten the right arm earlier on the downswing. However, you must maintain the angle between the wrist and forearm, otherwise your shots will go high and left with little power, a sure sign of over-correction and "casting" of the club head.

If your problem stems from the second swing fault, the correction process is completely different.

By starting the downswing too early with the hips, the swing becomes disconnected and the angle of attack becomes far too steep. To correct this, try to address the ball as usual, but then pull your right foot about 5 in (12.5 cm) back from the target line while ensuring that your hips and shoulders are still square to the ball-to-target line. This new stance will encourage a much more shallow attack on the ball and your swingpath will be much less severely in-to-out than before. This particular drill was used by Nick Price when he won the U.S. PGA Championship.

TIP

If your hips are moving too quickly on the downswing try one or both of these two tips. The first is one advocated by Nick Faldo and that is simply to curl your toes up at address just before you commence your backswing. The second is an old pro's remedy which is simply to practice with a golf ball under your left heel. This slows your hip turn on the downswing and gives your upper body time to catch up, which in turn encourages a shallower swingpath.

OTHER REASONS
FOR PUSHES AND HOOKS

✗ STANCE

Some hookers and pushers of the ball have a habit of standing too far away from the ball at address. This encourages too flat a backswing, almost "laid off" at the top of the swing (see right), that is, with the clubshaft pointing left of the target.

Try to avoid the feeling that you are stretching for the ball. At address, the arms should hang down comfortably and the butt end of the club should be 4 or 5 in (10 or 12 cm) from the inside of the left thigh.

Laid Off

✗ BACKSWING

Another cause of hooking is if you "hood," or close, the clubface on the backswing. This in turn encourages the left wrist to "bow" at the top of the swing and locks the clubface into a closed position on the downswing. From this position it is inevitable that you will hook the ball.

✓ To check for this fault, try starting your backswing slowly. After three feet (about 1 m) or so, stop the swing. If your left hand feels very much underneath the club and the clubface is still aiming toward the ball, then the clubface is closed and a

hook will follow. Try to allow the left forearm and the clubface to rotate clockwise a little on the backswing so that when the hands are midway between your knees and hips the clubshaft should be horizontal with the toe of the club pointing straight up. If you wear a watch on your left wrist, the watchface at this point should be parallel with the clubface.

Opposite: Jose Maria Olazabal concentrates on the flight of the ball.

CHAPTER THREE

Mis-Hits

This chapter is devoted to faulty swings and mis-hits and encompasses all of the truly embarrassing shots that golfers hate.

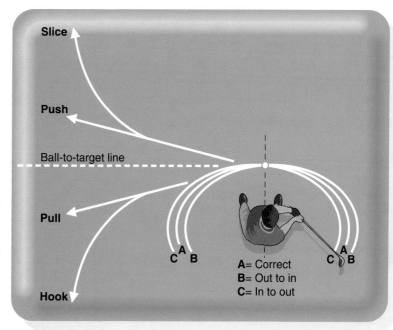

Here you will find the reasons and remedies for the main offenders: topping, where the ball fails to get off the ground altogether; chunking (or fluffing), you know the one, where the divot seems to go further than the ball; shanking, that heartbreaking shot that appears to come from nowhere; and skying, where the ball travels a greater distance upward than forward.

One point that always amuses me is that beginners seem to think that mis-hits only happen to them. Believe me, if you do not pay attentions to your swing basics any of the following faults can affect you, whether you are a beginner or a well-seasoned tournament professional.

TOPPING

Topping the ball is mostly associated with higher handicap golfers – but show me a golf professional who says he has never topped a shot and I will show you a liar! Even the best have gone through this awful golfing situation.

Topping the ball – hitting the ball above its equator – is truly embarrassing. There is nothing worse than putting all that effort into the swing and watching the ball scuttle 70 yards or less along the ground. Here are a few remedies to work on.

GRIP

Your grip may be much too tight at address, preventing you from properly cocking or hinging your wrists on the backswing and from releasing the clubhead at impact.

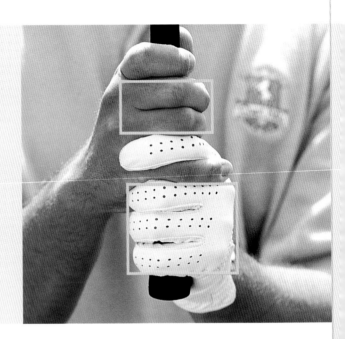

✓ CORRECTING GRIP
When holding the club, pressure should be light but firm and felt only in the last three fingers of the left hand and the middle two fingers of the right hand.

BALL POSITION

The ball may be too far forward in the stance or you may be too far away from it at address.

✓ CORRECTING BALL POSITION
The ball should always be at the bottom of your swing arc. For the shortest irons (pitching wedge or sand wedge), the ball for an average player should be opposite a point that is almost midway between the feet. With each longer club, the ball moves forward in the stance, that is, toward the target,

until, with the driver, it should be opposite the inside of your left heel. Athletic swingers will have the ball slightly farther forward in the stance with every club.

The distance a golfer stands from the ball depends on his height and build. A tall, athletic player will lean over from the hips more and thus stand closer to the ball. This will create a very upright swing. A shorter player will not lean over so much: he will stand farther away from the ball, thus creating a shallower, flatter swing. The butt end of the club should be no farther than 4 to 5 in (10 to 12 cm) from the inside of the left thigh.

STANCE

The problem may be that the player's body weight is set too much on the heels at address. This can cause the player to pull away from the ball at impact, pulling the club head up.

✔ CORRECTING STANCE

At the address position try to keep your weight on the balls of your feet and be sure not to rock back through the swing.

POSTURE

An inability to maintain a constant knee flex at address can cause the top half of the body to dip downward on the backswing. The only way to get the clubhead back to the ball is to make an opposing move on the downswing – that is, straightening the body up and away from the ball. Check that your posture is correct by looking at yourself sideways – in front of a mirror or a plate-glass window.

✔ REMEDY

You should be able to imagine a vertical line from the middle of your shoulders, down through the kneecaps and into the balls of your feet.

The only exception to this is a very tall player, who may have his shoulders over his toes.

BACKSWING

✗ Backswing

A common feature among "toppers" is poor transference of body weight throughout the swing. During a topper's backswing the hips tend to slide laterally to the right on the backswing instead of turning onto the right leg. This, in turn causes the shoulders to tilt instead of turning.

✗ Finish

As a result, the body's center of gravity is too much on the left side at the top of the swing, and the only way to get the clubface back somewhere near the ball is to reverse the process and slide the hips forward, leaving the center of gravity too much on the right side at impact.

✓ CORRECTING BACKSWING

The feeling you should develop is that on the backswing your left hip should turn toward the ball-to-target line and your right hip should move away from it. At the top of the backswing, your hips should have turned 40°, with the bulk of your weight on your right side and your chest balanced solidly over your right thigh.

This gives you enough time and space to transfer your weight correctly onto your left side on the downswing and finish with the majority of your weight over the left leg at the finish.

DOWNSWING

✗

A fault that is common to more experienced players is that the left hip clears (moves away from the ball-to-target line) too quickly at the start of the downswing and the left side accordingly "braces" (takes the finish position) too early, lifting the body up and away from the ball.

✓ CORRECTING DOWNSWING

Your downswing should commence with the feeling that your left shoulder and left hip are moving in unison. Try to concentrate on good tempo, and resist "jumping" at the ball.

FLUFFING (CHUNKING)

This, like the topped shot, is a truly embarrassing shot to experience. You stand up to the ball, ready to launch it 150 yards-plus to the target. You take your time over the shot, make what you feel is a strong, powerful swing and proceed to launch the ball all of 30 yards in the air!

Does this sound familiar to you? Then try these remedying measures.

GRIP

❌ The main reason for fluffing, or chunking, is normally poor grip pressure throughout the swing. Invariably the grip pressure at address is too weak in one or both hands.

   While you don't want to "white knuckle" your grip, if it is too loose the power in your body and arms won't transfer to the club or the ball.

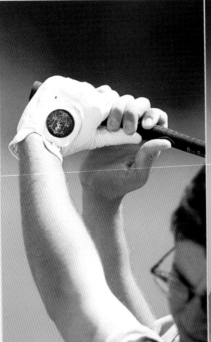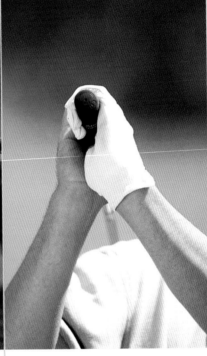

❌ At the top of the backswing, the palm of the right hand comes away from the grip.

❌ More commonly, the last three fingers on the left hand start to uncurl.

   Both faults will cause the backswing to over-extend and, instead of the clubshaft pointing to a spot parallel to the ball-to-target line, the club will be pointing down toward the ground.

✔ CORRECTING GRIP

The last thing I would recommend to anyone is to grip the club tightly, but it is important to have a secure hold of the golf club. When I say secure I mean not only how the fingers are placed on the handle, but also the amount of pressure applied.

> **TIP**
>
> Remember, if you grip the club too tightly, you will prevent the natural cocking or hinging of the wrists in the backswing; too tight a grip may also tend to engender tension in the arms and shoulders, making a smooth movement impossible.

✔ If you find that the palm of your right hand is coming away from the shaft at the top of the backswing, then most of the blame can be placed on poor positioning of the right thumb on the grip. The right thumb should be touching the base of the forefinger (ideally, the middle joint of the thumb should be touching the knuckle of the forefinger). The thumb itself should run slightly down the left side of the grip (as viewed from the address position).

✔ Alternatively, the pressure on the grip may be too light. Try to apply a little more pressure in the last three fingers of the left hand and the middle two fingers of the right hand.

BALL POSITION

✕ Poor positioning of the ball in relation to stance is the one fault that occurs throughout a golfer's career regardless of his general standard of play. It is a common fault responsible for causing, or exaggerating the effects of, many other swing faults.

✓ CORRECTING BALL POSITION

When playing iron shots, the ball should be positioned slightly farther back in your stance to ensure that you strike the ball just before your swing bottoms out. This encourages you to hit the ball first, and then take a divot. With a wood shot, you play the ball farther forward in your stance so that you strike the ball at the bottom of your swing arc or even slightly forward of that.

If the ball is too far forward, especially with iron shots, you are likely to hit the ground first and the ball second, and the result is a fluffed or smothered shot. In a good iron shot, the divot will appear an inch or so *nearer* to the target than the original position of the ball.

STANCE

✕ Sometimes you will find that your hands are too far behind the ball at address. This fault is most often seen with wood shots and normally affects the experienced player.

If the hands are too far behind the ball at address, the whole backswing is put out of sync. It also allows the hands to be overactive throughout the swing and promotes an early release of the clubhead on the downswing, thus creating an "early hit."

Coupled with this, the player will often be standing far too close to the ball and will therefore be too cramped at address. This will force the player's body to get in the way of the hands and arms in the downswing and invariably the club once again hits the ground before the ball, causing a fluffed, heavy or "fat" shot.

> **TIP**
> I cannot emphasize enough the importance of ball positioning in the stance. Some golfers feel that by moving the ball back in their stance they will overcome the problem of fluffing. I find that the majority of players who have poor hand positioning should concentrate on curing that fault, rather than altering what may be a perfect ball position.

✔ CORRECTING STANCE

Whichever club you use, at address the hands should be in line with your left ear and opposite the inside of your left thigh.

▶ DRILL

To ensure that you are not standing too close to the ball at address, make certain that you can pass the flat of your hand through the gap between the butt-end of the club and your left thigh. If you can't, step back slightly.

POSTURE

✖ Too Erect

Have you noticed when watching a professional golfer how consistent his swing is, regardless of how far he is trying to hit the ball, and whichever club he is using? The head is relatively still (but not completely), and the shoulders, arms, hands and clubhead move back and forth on a consistent, repetitive swingpath, all adding up to consistently good ball strike.

One of the reasons professionals (and good amateurs) achieve consistent strikes is that they have the right set of body angles at address.

✖ Too Crouched

In other words, they have a relatively straight back with their bottom sticking out and the right amount of knee flex.

Someone who is fluffing a fair number of shots will usually have poor posture. They either sit back with a curved spine or stoop over the ball. This causes the upper body to move up or down on the backswing. In order to get the club back to the ball there has to be a compensating move on the downswing. Mis-time the compensating move and a fluffed or chunked shot, or even a topped one, results.

✔ CORRECTING POSTURE

I have already covered posture in the chapter on pulls and slices, but I want to reiterate the points I made there, in a slightly different form.

Stand erect, approximately 2 feet (60 cm) away from the ball with your heels shoulder-width apart. Looking down at your feet, you should be able to see your shoelaces. Now bend your knees until you can no longer see the laces.

Gripping the club with both hands, hold it out in front of you at shoulder height. Now lower the club down until the butt of the club is facing toward your waist but the clubshaft is still horizontal to the ground.

Now bend forward from the hips (not the waist) sticking your tailbone out and keeping your lower back straight. The clubhead should now be touching the ground and your body weight should be on the balls of your feet (but not on the toes).

Finally, your chin should be held clear of your chest, both arms should be soft (neither weak nor rigidly straight) and your right elbow and right shoulder should be slightly lower than their left counterparts.

A helpful tip to check that you have correct posture is to look at your right-side reflection in a mirror or large pane of glass. If you have the correct posture, you should be able to run a vertical line through the balls of your feet, up through your kneecaps and finishing in your shoulder. For taller players, the weight should still rest in the balls of the feet but the shoulder line should be more over the toes.

BACKSWING

 Probably the most common swing fault is the reverse pivot – the failure to transfer one's weight correctly on the backswing and have to make a compensating move on the downswing.

1 The body weight stays on the left side on the backswing.

2 The body weight moves to the right side on the downswing, rather than shift from the right on the backswing to the left on the downswing. Thus the power on your swing is on the wrong side of your body.

This reverse movement encourages the golfer to "cast" the clubhead (release it early) on the downswing and this in turn increases the chances of fluffing or chunking (hitting the ball heavy).

CORRECTING YOUR BACKSWING

In my experience, correcting a reverse pivot is quite simple. As your shoulders are turning on the backswing, try to get your chest moving so that at the top of the swing it is over your right thigh. If you have completed this move correctly you should feel pressure in the right thigh as the bulk of your body weight has now moved onto the right side of your body. Your body weight should then move across to the left on the downswing and follow-through. Think of your body weight pulling the clubface as you swing.

DOWNSWING

❌ Early Release

Early release, otherwise known as casting the clubhead, is a fault associated with golfers who feel that they need to encourage the ball to get in the air and also with players who "hit from the top." An early release (hitting from the top) occurs when the hands throw the club out away from the body during the start of the downswing. The back of the right hand and the angle it has with the clubshaft straightens too early and the result is almost a scooping action in which the left wrist is cupped at impact and what little divot you have taken is up to 6 in (15 cm) behind the ball.

You may also find that because of the "sweeping" type of action required to hit wood shots, you hit your woods better from the tee than from the fairway.

✔ Late Hit

Many of you will have seen either slow-motion videotapes or sequential photography of top professionals hitting shots. What you will notice is that at least halfway through the downswing they manage to retain the same angle between the back of the right hand and the clubshaft that they had at the top of the backswing. This is commonly referred to as a late hit.

✓ CORRECTING DOWNSWING

To overcome early release, you need to retain that clubshaft-left arm angle for as long as possible. A drill that is useful for beginners and experienced players alike is the following. This is a drill that can be used on the golf course as well as the range, but do *not* hit balls while practising !!

Grip   **Backswing**   **Downswing**

1 Stand in the address position but grip the club with the right hand at the top of the clubshaft. Then place the left hand on the shaft below, separated from the right hand. When looking down make sure you can see two or three knuckles on the left hand.

2 and 3 Now make some swings concentrating on backswings and downswings but making little if any follow-through. At first you will still try to "cast" the club from the top and you will feel your right wrist and left forearm touching each other

halfway down. This is showing you where the releasing point of your downswing is occurring. The quieter you make your hands at the start of the downswing, and the longer you retain the angle between the back of the left hand and the clubshaft, the closer to the hitting zone this knocking effect will occur; and you may eliminate it completely.

Try to use the whole body on the downswing: it is very easy to concentrate on just the arms, but this will only hinder your development.

▶ DRILL

Here's a useful drill that can be used anywhere, including the home or office. This will encourage you to keep your wrists cocked during the backswing and downswing.

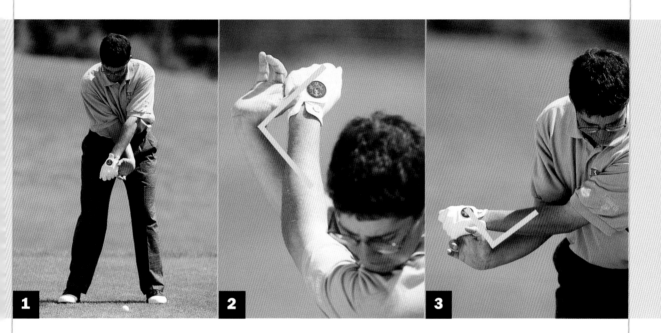

1 **2** **3**

▶ **1 and 2** Assume an address position but cross your left wrist over your right. Now with your left hand take hold of the forefinger and middle finger of your right hand and bend them back as far as you can without hurting yourself. The angle you have now created between the right forearm and the back of the right hand is the one that you want to retain for as long as possible on the downswing.

3 Now take some practice swings trying to keep that angle for as long as you can.

TIP

For experienced players, it is good to swing from the top of the backswing by pulling the club down with the left hand into the back of the ball. They should also feel that they are hitting the ball with the butt of the club. These two remedies are certainly useful, but to overdo them can cause a player to get "trapped" on the downswing and encounter some downswing problems so should not be overused.

SHANKING

The shank is probably the most demoralizing and destructive shot in golf. In fact, I have heard of people giving up playing golf simply because they could not find a cure for it. The very mention of the word is enough to send shivers down spines and start people shanking. It could even be argued that shanking is contagious!

The shank is a shot that, for a right-handed golfer, flies straight out to the right and sometimes gives the appearance (although it is not possible) of flying at right angles to the ball-to-target line. It happens when the ball is struck in the area of the hosel, the hollow socket where the bottom of the shaft is joined to the clubhead. It is usually caused by the clubface closing, or hooding, on either an in-to-out swingpath or, alternatively, on an extreme out-to-in swingpath. In both cases the hands at impact are farther away from the body than they were at address.

Some people have argued that shanking is caused only by an open clubface at impact, but this has been proved not to be the case. Others believe that addressing the ball with the toe, rather than the center, of the clubface, will alleviate the problem. In the short term it might, but long term your swing will re-adjust and you will have only exaggerated the problem.

There are several causes of shanking, these being the most common ones.

GRIP

✗ Shanking is caused by one of two things. Either the grip pressure is too tight and the grip is too strong – hooker's grip – or the right hand is too much on top. The misplaced right hand is the more problematic. It encourages the hands to roll open the clubface on the backswing and leads to a very flat backswing. From this position a good player will attack the ball from the inside, trying to roll the clubface back to square at impact. The high handicapper with a flat backswing will throw the club out at the top of the downswing, causing an exaggerated out-to-in swingpath, once again trying to square up the clubface at impact.

✔ CORRECTING YOUR GRIP

To start with, it is important to adopt a "neutral" grip. Place your left hand next to the grip so that the club runs along a line drawn from just above the base of the little finger across the other fingers to the middle joint of the forefinger. Now close your left hand around the grip. Looking down you should be able to see 2 or 3 knuckles – no more and certainly no less. With the middle joint of the thumb touching the knuckle of the forefinger, a line should be formed between the two. This line should point to an area halfway between your chin and right shoulder.

The right hand should be placed on the shaft in such a way that the line formed between thumb and forefinger once again points to an area between the chin and right shoulder.

Pull grip
(see page 13)

Slicer's grip
(see page 13)

TIP

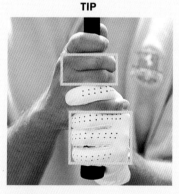

The only pressure felt in the grip should be in the last three fingers of the left hand and the middle two fingers of the right hand.

Neutral grip
(see page 31)

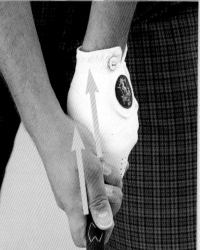

BALL POSITION

❌ Often, a shanker will have placed the ball too far back in his stance, which encourages a very in-to-out swing.

✔️ **CORRECTING BALL POSITION**
I like to see more experienced players with the ball opposite the left heel for a wood shot, and moving back gradually to a position just short of midway between the feet for a short iron. The less experienced or less flexible players should have the ball positioned for a wood 1 in (2.5 cm) inside the left heel moving back to midway between the feet for short irons.

ALIGNMENT

❌ Poor body alignment requires a compensating move to avoid shanking. If the line through the feet and shoulders is aiming to the left of target, this encourages the player to take the club back outside the ball-to-target line. This in turn causes the hands to be farther away from the body at the top of the backswing than at address. Unless a compensating move occurs on the downswing, the clubface will remain farther away from the body and the hosel will be too close to the ball at impact, resulting in a shank.

✔️ **CORRECTING YOUR ALIGNMENT**
The line through your feet, hips and shoulders must always be parallel to the ball-to-target line (the only exception to this rule is in the short game). You will find it useful when practicing, to place a club on the ground parallel to the ball-to-target line and align your feet with the club's shaft.

> **TIP**
> Always remember that, regardless of what shape you are in and whatever your age, golf is an athletic pursuit and as such it is only right that you assume an "athletic" state of readiness. In other words, obtain good posture.

POSTURE

❌ Shankers may have poor posture, which causes them to move their weight forward onto their toes instead of the balls of their feet during the backswing. This results in the clubface and hands moving away from the body and out of the swingpath. It is inevitable that on the downswing the hands and clubhead will remain too far away from the body, resulting in a shank.

CORRECTING YOUR POSTURE

Stand upright, with your feet shoulder-width apart and a club by your side. Now bend forward from the hips, keeping your chin off your chest. Ensure that your rear end, or tailbone, is sticking out slightly. Now let your hands and arms hang down comfortably and bend your knees slightly.

Your body weight should be centered over the balls of your feet. Now grip the club, keeping approximately 4 to 5 in (10 to 12 cm) between the butt end of the club and your inner thigh. Your arms should be comfortably straight, but not locked rigid, and the right shoulder and right elbow should be only slightly below their left hand counterparts.

BACKSWING

X It amazes some players how on one shot they will hook the ball, or at the least draw it, and the next shot can be a shank that goes in a completely opposite direction. In fact, I would go so far as to say that many good players who put hook spin on the ball can have a problem with shanking.

The problem lies with the first few feet of the backswing. Instead of having a good one-piece backswing in which the club, left arm, left shoulder, and waist move together, the hands initiate the backswing by rolling open the clubface. This pushes the butt of the club away from the body, with the clubface coming too far inside the ball-to-target line and "inside" the hands, encouraging a very flat backswing. The only way to get the clubface back to square at impact is to roll the clubface back to its original position. Overdo this and the clubface will be hooded or closed, and the shot will be a hook or, if the butt of the club is still farther away from the body than it was at address, a shank.

X Clubface inside hands

✓ CORRECTING YOUR BACKSWING
At the start of the backswing, the left forearm should rotate slightly away from the ball but it should also be synchronized with the body turn. The backswing's turning action will move the clubhead slightly inside the ball-to-target line, but at the same time it should remain "outside" the hands.

Clubface outside hands

Instead of the clubface initiating the backswing, try to imagine that the butt end of the club starts the backswing and that you are trying to brush your right thigh with the club during the first few feet of the swing. This encourages the clubhead to stay "outside" the hands at the start and move only just inside the ball-to-target line.

 DRILL

Address an imaginary ball with your hands sliding down the shaft and the butt of the club sticking into your waist. Now make a few very short practice swings going back on your backswing approximately two to three feet (one-half to one meter). This will help encourage a one-piece backswing.

SKYING

A skied shot usually occurs when using a wood off the tee or off a very "fluffy" lie in the rough, where the ball is sitting up. It is the result of a sharp descending blow that sees the clubhead go almost completely underneath the ball at impact. The resulting shot usually goes high into the air but does not travel a very great distance.

GRIP

The most common cause of skying is the grip, which will usually be a hooker's grip, with both hands too far underneath the shaft. If you look down at your grip you would probably have at least 4 knuckles showing on the left hand.

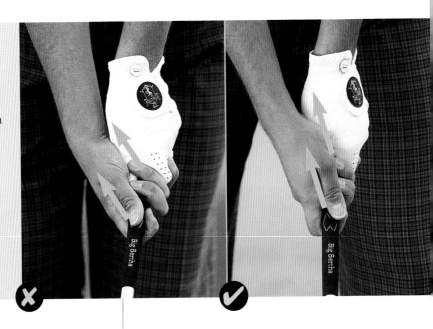

X This strong grip encourages the golfer to lift the club up very quickly on the backswing with little turning of the shoulders and body.

With no width to the backswing, the legs, hips and shoulders have neither time nor space to bring the club back onto the correct swingpath. This results in a sharp descending blow, often taking a divot.

✔ CORRECTING YOUR GRIP

Hold the club with a neutral grip (see page 31) by trying to get both hands more on top of the shaft. With a neutral grip you would you look down at your hands and note that:

- only two knuckles are visible on the back of the left hand.
- the line created between the thumb and forefinger on the left hand is pointing up to a point midway between the chin and right shoulder, and
- when the right hand is placed on the grip, the corresponding line between the thumb and forefinger should also point to an area midway between your chin and right shoulder.

If one or both of the thumb/forefinger lines point at your right shoulder, or outside it, the grip is still too strong.

POSTURE

❌ If a player stands too close to the ball at address and consequently stands too tall, then he will be unable to turn back on the correct swingpath. He will then be unable to create the width necessary for the sweeping downswing that is required when hitting wood shots from the tee. Rather, the swing action is all hands and arms with very little movement from the body. The shoulders rarely turn, in fact they are more likely to tilt. This particular fault is common not only to beginners and high handicappers but also to senior golfers who may be unable to turn away from the ball properly.

✅ **CORRECTING POSTURE**

When addressing the ball, try to leave 4 to 5 in (10 to 12 cm) between the butt of the club and the inside of your left thigh. You may now feel that you are reaching too far for the ball. If so, it means that you are still standing too tall. Check that your posture is not too upright, that the knees are flexed slightly, the upper body is leaning forward from the hips with a relatively straight back, and your rear end is sticking out slightly. You may need to step back from the ball a bit. The mental picture one should have for correct posture is the position you would be in if you were just about to sit on a high stool (keep your weight on the balls of your feet).

CHAPTER FOUR

Short Game and Putting Problems

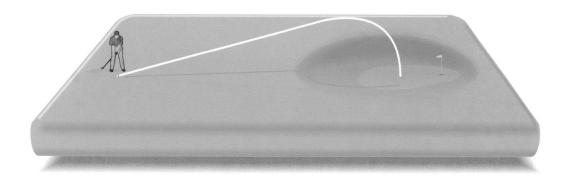

I remember a former boss of mine, Mike Barton, telling me how as a young tournament professional he got a sound beating by Australian golfer Rodger Davis in the televised Penfold PGA Matchplay championship. When I asked Mike what the main difference was between the two of them, he said: "Very little off the tee." If anything, Mike felt that he was the better ball-striker. The real difference was when Davis got to within 140 yards of the green. Apparently it was like darts: he was arrow straight and rarely failed to get up and down in two.

The short game is the one aspect that is most often practiced by top tournament professionals. Take the hint! In this chapter I have changed the order of fault finding because I want to concentrate on the more common problems you will face. Later on, I'll offer a variety of tips and drills that will help your short game and lower your scores.

I will also look at the make-or-break area of the game, putting, which has been the arena for some of the most famous victories and defeats in the game.

CHIPPING

 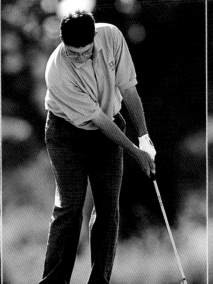 

 A chip shot is a short low-running shot, usually played to the green. Chip shots are often inconsistent – either too clean and long or too heavy and short, due to a very "wristy" downswing and follow-through. This is where the left wrist is "cupped" and the back of the left hand is pointing up at the sky.

This is a fault common to weekend golfers, who feel that they have to help the ball up into the air, instead of letting the loft of the club do the work.

 ## CORRECTING A CHIP SHOT

At address the ball should be set back in your stance, which encourages your hands to be ahead of the ball. This hand position is one which you must retain throughout the swing for short chip shots. Keep your weight on your left side all the time and try to develop the feeling that you are hitting the ball with the back of the left hand while just brushing the grass underneath the clubhead.

▶ DRILL

Here's one of my favorite drills for dealing with cupping the left wrist when playing short chips.

If you can get hold of an old golf shaft, stick it down the butt end of an old eight iron. Now take up your chipping stance. Make a few strokes trying to keep the back of your left hand square to the target on the follow-through. If you fail to do so, you will get a gentle reminder as the protruding golf shaft "tickles" your ribs. This drill exaggerates the required action but it will help cure the problem.

CHIPPING WITH MID-IRONS

✗ Inability to judge distances can be caused by failure to assess where the ball will land with each club. Too many amateur golfers look at and focus on where they want the ball to finish and not, more importantly, where the ball should land before running up to the hole.

✓ CORRECT CHIPPING

To be able to land shots strategically you need to know which club to use and how the ball will react with a particular club. Always remember to keep the ball on the ground as much as possible when chipping.

The following suggestions are made anticipating a clean lie and a relatively flat green.

A 5-iron ball should spend about 10% of the distance in the air and 90% rolling to the hole.

A 7-iron ball should spend about 25% of the distance in the air

A 9-iron ball should spend about 50% of the distance in the air

The key factors are that, whichever club you use, you should grip down the shaft to the same spot on every club and use the same swing tempo. Learn to let the club's loft work for you.

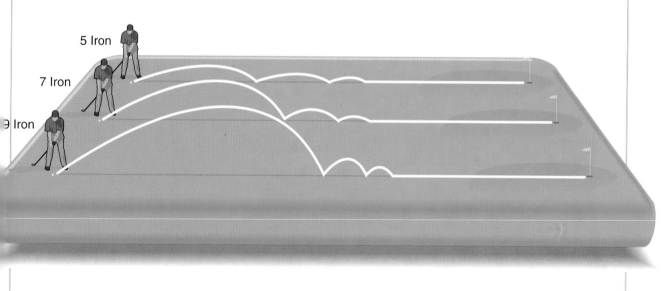

5 Iron

7 Iron

9 Iron

PITCHING

Pitching involves the "in-between" shots that range from about 10 to 100 yards. Neither a full shot nor a chip shot, a pitch shot is one of the most important swings of your game alongside chipping and putting. I think it was Gary Player who said that 70% of all shots in a round of golf are within 70 yards of the green.

"Today you can drive up to the average country club practice area and see about three dinosaurs for every golfer who's out there working on pitch and run shots"

Lee Trevino

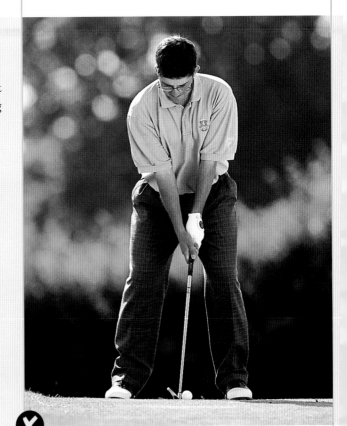

Normal stance

INCONSISTENT PITCHING

Before the majority of my students had come to me, they had failed to realize just how important a part of the game pitching is. Consequently they had not shown it the respect it deserves, and practiced it. Very often these players would try to treat it as a normal shot and address the ball as they would if they were intending to hit the ball

150 yards or more. The problems with this are twofold: first, the backswing becomes too long, and to compensate the player has to decelerate on the downswing sacrificing accuracy; and second, the lower body gets in the way at impact, compromising accuracy and distance.

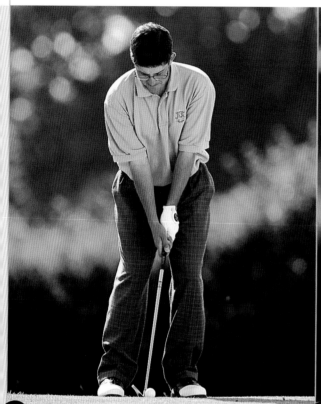

Pitching stance (face on)

Pitching stance (side on)

CORRECT PITCHING

Address the ball as normal but with a slightly narrower stance. Now draw your left foot back a little from the ball-to-target line. This opens up your lower body in relation to the ball-to-target line. This, in turn, will ensure that your legs are fairly passive while making sure that they are out of the way at impact. It is, however, vital that the clubface and your shoulders are square in relation to the ball-to-target line, otherwise you will pull your pitch shots left of target.

The ball should be positioned slightly forward of the middle of your stance, and the butt end of the club opposite the inner half of your left thigh.

About two-thirds of your body weight at address should be on your left side, and both knees should be flexed slightly toward the target as if you were trying to mirror the impact position.

The follow-through should be the same length as the backswing. In fact, it should be a mirror image of the backswing.

SHANKING

✗ Shanking and pulling the ball left of target are both caused by swinging the club on an incorrect swingpath. This is normally caused by rolling the clubface open on the backswing in a mistaken attempt to obtain a higher trajectory. This pushes the hands farther away from the body than they were at address, causing a flat swingpath. If you do not make a compensating move on the downswing, a shank will follow; if you over-compensate, you will probably pull the ball left of target.

✓ CORRECTING SHANKING

Because of the relative shortness of a pitch swing, the normal cure for shanking full shots does not apply here. It is much easier to concentrate on the following drill.

Take your normal pitching stance as already described (see page 71). If your stance and posture are right, then simply work on the feeling that at the halfway stage of your backswing, your thumbs should be pointing up at the sky and not behind you (above left). On the follow-through this position should be repeated. I like to call this the "thumbs-up" routine (above right).

LOB SHOTS

❌ Hitting the ball a short distance with a high trajectory might appear to be very simple but the lob shot is often a poorly played and misunderstood shot feared by many golfers. Too often, the shot is thinned (hit too cleanly) and flies on a very low trajectory straight into the hazard you were trying to avoid. This is due to the golfer's misunderstanding of how to play the shot: instead of allowing the club to do the work, the golfer tries to help the ball up into the air by scooping it up, but only succeeds in making contact with the bottom edge of the clubface which sends the ball straight out rather than up and out.

✔ CORRECTING LOB SHOTS

The lob shot should only be played from a lie where there is an adequate carpet of grass underneath. Address the ball with the line through your feet, hips and shoulders aiming left of the target (an open aim). The ball should be positioned farther forward than normal. I like to see the ball at a point somewhere near the toe of the golfer's left foot. The clubface should be aiming just to the right of the ball-to-target line. The grip should be slightly weakened – in other words, rather like a slicer's grip, with both hands more toward the top of the shaft than normal.

Now make a swing that is fairly long and is parallel to your open stance – but *not* parallel to the ball-to-target line. The swing speed should be "quiet", but accelerate smoothly into the ball. It is imperative that the hands do not square up to the clubface through impact.

A good tip I learned from Tom Watson was to get the feeling on the follow-through that the knuckles on the left hand are pointing skyward. This helps the clubface remain open through impact.

BUNKER PLAY

EXPLOSION (SPLASH) SHOTS

Throughout my playing career, I have had to play in innumerable pro-ams, celebrity events, and charity golf days. In most of these events I have had to play with three amateur golfers on my team. The one thing that has continued to amaze me about my amateur playing partners is that, regardless of their experience and expertise, very few of them actually have any idea how to play a conventional bunker "explosion" or "splash" shot. Ask yourself how often you or any of your playing partners get out of a bunker and finish close to the hole. Read on and you will find some of the more common faults in bunker play that I have witnessed over the years.

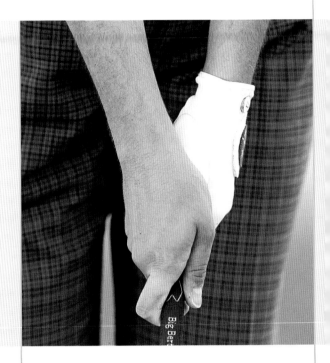

When trying to play conventional bunker "explosion" or "splash" shots there is no consistency in the results: too long or too short, you take too much or too little sand, and too often you fail entirely to get the ball out of the bunker.

All these problems are caused by not knowing the required technique. I've lost count of the number of times I've seen amateurs trying to play bunker shots exactly as they would play a conventional pitch shot. Very often the ball is too far back in the stance, the clubface is square, and the swing has much in common with a heavyweight boxing match: short and violent.

✓ CORRECTING EXPLOSION (SPLASH) SHOTS

When playing an "explosion" shot, remember that it is the only golf shot where you are trying to *not* make direct contact with the ball! The idea is to encourage the ball to ride out of the bunker on a wedge of sand. To do this, you must have sound technique. Stand in the bunker with the line across your feet, hips, and shoulders aiming to the left of the ball-to-target line (open stance). The clubface is square to the ball-to-target line, thus open in relation to your stance. The ball should be farther forward in your stance than normal: I like to see it opposite the left heel and toes. The grip should be a little weak with both hands more on top of the club to prevent the clubface turning over at impact.

1 Now shuffle your feet into the sand. This achieves three things:
- It gives you a firm base to swing from;
- You will be able to feel the quality and depth of sand;
- It lowers your swingpath, helping you hit the sand before the ball.

2 Now focus on a spot 2 to 3 in (5 to 7 cm) before the ball and make a nice full, rhythmical swing in line with your open stance, *not* with the ball-to-target line.

Make sure that you accelerate through the ball and don't quit on it. Also ensure that the clubface remains open in relation to the swingpath. I like to think of the clubface aiming at the sky on the follow-through. If you are using a sand wedge and you manage to keep the clubface open, you should take a nice long shallow divot.

TIP
Always look at the spot on the sand where you want the clubhead to enter. Never look at the ball. Allow the length of your swing to control the distance you want the ball to go.

PLUGGED OR BURIED BUNKER SHOTS

We have all experienced the disappointment when our ball pitches into a bunker and we find it buried in the sand. How do you play this shot? Do you hit it like a normal "explosion" or "splash" shot? Do you hit it harder? Do you have to change your set-up?

All these questions put doubt into your mind. This in turn breeds indecision, which means you cannot be positive with the stroke. To be less than positive with bunker shots means you will be playing a lot of them, because you will never get out!

✔ PLAYING PLUGGED SHOTS

If the ball is lying deeper in the sand than normal, a bigger and deeper divot has to be taken. The golfer has to remember at all times: the sand wedge is designed to "bounce" in the sand and take a long but shallow divot. To overcome this, the player needs to make adjustments not only to his set-up but also slight adjustments to his swing.

The clubface should be square (or even slightly closed) to the ball-to-target line. The line through the feet, hips, and shoulders should be parallel to the ball-to-target line (much as they would be for a normal fairway shot).

But the most important factor to remember is ball position: it is imperative that it be opposite the middle of your stance. This pushes your hands much farther in front of the ball. Coupled with two-thirds of your body weight being on your left side, your forward hand position encourages the steep backswing needed to take a deep divot.

As with the "explosion" or "splash" bunker shot, do not look directly at the ball but at a spot 2 to 3 in (5 to 7 cm) before it.

It also helps to cock the wrists a little earlier in the backswing, and to remember to be aggressive on the downswing. There will be little if any follow-through as the sand will rob the clubhead of its momentum. The ball itself will come out low with no backspin, so make allowances for extra run on the ball. Be bold but do not overshoot.

You may find hitting plugged balls out of sand a lot easier if you use a pitching wedge or even a 9-iron. The reason for this is that the sand wedge is designed with a special rounded sole that forces the club to "bounce" through the sand, taking a shallow divot. On the other hand, the pitching wedge has a sharp leading edge that will dig into the sand.

PLAYING UPHILL AND DOWNHILL BUNKER SHOTS

✘

The majority of amateur golfers really struggle with these shots and although professionals are not normally worried by having to play bunker shots, uphill and downhill lies leave even the best pros thinking twice.

Golfers have a tendency to treat uphill and downhill lies as if they were normal bunker shots off an even lie. This attitude can result in never

getting out of the bunker. With an uphill lie, the clubhead gets stuck in the upslope on the follow-through, with the ball traveling no distance at all. With the downhill lie, the clubhead normally bounces off the sand too early in the downswing and hits the ball too cleanly. (In fact I have actually seen people miss the ball entirely.)

✔ CORRECTING UPHILL BUNKER SHOTS

Address the ball as normal, with the ball positioned where it would be for a conventional "explosion" or "splash" shot. Now lean on your right leg until you feel that about three-quarters of your body weight is on your right side. This should encourage your right shoulder to dip down so that the line through your shoulders is parallel to the slope. The swing itself should follow the contour of the slope with the golfer aiming for a powerful impact position that forces the club out of the sand, achieving some degree of follow-through. Bear in mind that this shot will come out fairly high with very little roll, so try to be bold.

✔ CORRECTING DOWNHILL BUNKER SHOTS

The ball should be positioned back past the middle of your stance with most of your body weight on the left leg. This time your right shoulder will be above the left shoulder and the line through the shoulders should be parallel to the slope.

The swing for this type of lie is very much a hands-and-arms movement, and I like to see the stance just a bit wider than normal; this helps to keep the body passive.

I like to think of the swing being L-shaped: a fairly abrupt lifting of the club with the hands and arms on the backswing, and a long and low follow-through. Be sure to hit the sand first and allow for considerable run of the ball when it hits the green.

PUTTING

"Lord, give me strength to hole a putt,
So that even I, When telling of it to my friends,
May never need to lie."

I found this simple prayer for putting etched on a piece of wood at a jumble sale when I was 11 years old. It really caught my attention. Who it is by and when it was composed, I do not know. What I do know is that many people have muttered a similar prayer many times on the course. People fail to appreciate that, on average, 43% of a better player's strokes in a round of golf are on the green! As Harry Vardon once said, "Putting is a game within a game."

I have selected some of the more common faults found on the putting green and described the necessary remedies. Nothing, however, will improve your putting if you do not practice!

Jack Nicklaus says that the set up for his individual putting style involves keeping his eyes over the ball, which helps him to keep the clubface square and on line. This makes him appear to crouch over the ball more than other professionals.

INCONSISTENT STROKE

❌ A very inconsistent stroke that results in all-around poor putting and poor scoring. This is due to the player not having a consistent set up routine coupled with a poor conception of how the putter should be swung.

▶ Whenever you watch top-flight professional golf, be it women's, seniors or full PGA Tour golf, you will notice that each player has his or her unique putting style. Some, like Jack Nicklaus, crouch over the ball (see above); others, like Ben Crenshaw and Justin Leonard, stand more upright. But however they stand, there are some rules to which they all adhere.

GRIP

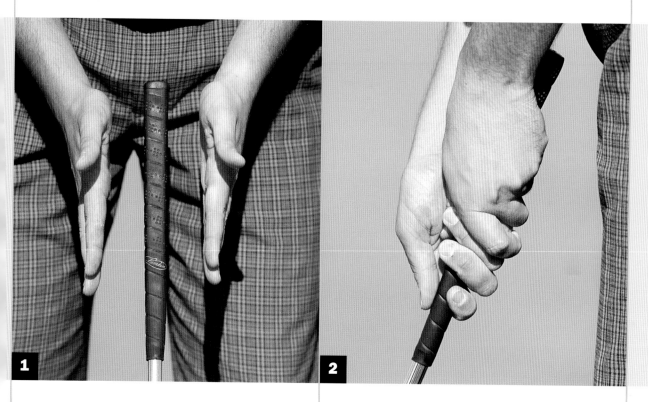

1

2

CORRECTING YOUR GRIP

Putting styles may vary, but you will find with all good players that the lower body does not move at all during the putting stroke.

Most players bend from the waist so that their hands and arms can hang freely. The putter face is aimed directly at the target.

1 The grip can be varied but I always like to see the palms of the hands facing each other and square to the putter face.

2 For putting, I always try to promote a reverse overlap grip where the index finger of the left hand overlaps the right hand "pinkie" or little finger. Your hold on the club should be light, and I like to see the club grip high up in the palm of the left hand. Both of these points help to "quiet" the hands while the putting stroke is made. As you stand at address, the ball should be positioned at a point directly underneath your left eyeball, and when your eyes look down they should be in line with the ball-to-target line. The putting stroke should be a pendulum-like action involving the shoulders and arms but with very little involvement from the hands or wrists. Always remember that the length of your stroke dictates how far the ball travels. Do not try to hit the ball hard or soft as in time this will have a detrimental effect on your putting stroke. Putting is a controlled stroke that has nothing to do with power or strength.

PUTTING TEMPO

Putting problems are usually caused by deceleration of the putter head on the forward swing. Most golfers have little difficulty hitting the ball more or less along the correct line but many find it very difficult to hit it the right distance. All great putters have a great sense of tempo and keep the same rhythm regardless of the length or complexity of the putt they are playing.

✔ CORRECT PUTTING TEMPO

The distance you hit your putts, if controlled rather than lucky, are dictated by the length of your stroke, including a good follow-through. The key to avoiding deceleration of the putter head is to ensure that your follow-through is twice as long as your backswing. The putter head should be accelerating through the ball.

▶ A drill I like to use is one that "deadens" the hands and encourages the shoulders to "rock." Simply put a club across your chest and under your armpits. Holding the club in place with your upper arms, try to hit some putts. You will replicate in an obvious way how your shoulders and arms should move while putting, and you should also note how passive your hands are.

DRILL

Next time you are practicing your putting, try this useful drill. When addressing the ball on a flat part of the green, place a ball on the ground 8 in (20 cm) behind the first. Now try to hit the target ball without hitting the "backstop" ball. Be sure that the transition between backswing and forward swing is not jerky but rather like a pendulum and that the follow-through is twice the length of the backswing.

Address

Backswing

Forward stroke and contact

TIP
You should always allow for more or less break depending on the speed of the greens. Generally, dry fast greens will see the putt break more, and wet slow greens will see the putt break less.

THE YIPS

❌ The basic cause of the yips is a "mental" fear of missing the hole, which manifests itself in an uncontrolled reflex action by the hands. The strange thing is that many golfers who suffer from this problem are good long-range putters: because few are expected to hole long puts, they feel under less pressure. But although the yips arise from, and are nourished by, pressure-induced fear, most cases can be cured quite simply – by developing a sound technique.

✓ MENTAL PREPARATION

First of all let us address the mental side of the equation. As Dr Gary Wiren noted, "The fear of missed putts comes from having missed putts in the past and over-remembering the misses." This is where over-thinking the game can cause problems.

To overcome this, try to put things into perspective. You will always miss more putts than you make; and, if you *do* miss, will the world as we know it end tomorrow? I doubt it. Now start to believe in yourself and start to think that you will hole the putt instead of thinking in a negative pattern. Always *will* the ball into the hole.

❌ The true source of the yips is most likely poor technique. Very often a player suffering from the yips will grip the putter too tightly, stand too near to or too far from the ball, aim incorrectly, and make a "wristy" type of stroke. To overcome this, the golfer needs to lock his wrists (without getting too tense) and prevent the left wrist from "cupping" at impact.

✓ PHYSICAL PREPARATION

First try to ensure that the putter grip is held as high up in your left hand as possible. I like to see the handle come up between the fleshy parts at the base of the hand.

This will arch your left wrist and lock it. Now place your right hand on the grip, ensuring that the palms of both hands are square to the target and facing each other. The grip you make is, of course, up to you, but I strongly favor the reverse overlap, where the index finger of the left hand overlaps the little finger of the right hand.

If you should find that the left wrist is still cupping at impact then a reverse grip would be advisable. The simplest version has the right hand

▼ PRO-WATCHING ▼

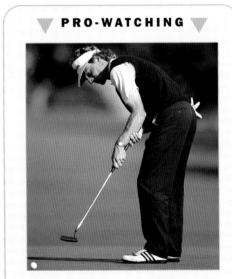

Bernhard Langer putted with his famed long reverse grip which he perfected before having long-handled putters specially made for him.

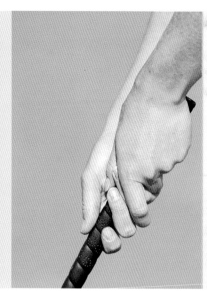  

Reverse Overlap   **Reverse Grip**   **Long Reverse Grip**

is at the top of the grip and the left hand is below. This grip has been used a lot by golfers such as Fred Couples. If problems still persist then the long reverse grip would be advisable. This is where the left hand is separated from the right hand and the right hand holds the left forearm to the shaft. This style was advocated for many years by Bernhard Langer. Whichever grip you decide to use, keep your hold of the club light.

A key factor when missing short putts is ball position. The majority of good, consistent putters have the ball positioned directly under their left eye and over the ball-to-target line. If you stand too far away from the ball or too near it, you will encourage an inconsistent stroke and you will be more apt to push or pull your putts.

Many players aim the putter head incorrectly, usually when a player takes his stance first and then aligns the putter head. All of the great putters aim the putter first and *then* take their stance.

Try to relax over the ball and swing the putter head smoothly with a regular tempo rather than with a quick, jerky swing. Relax your wrists to keep tension from starting in your hands, moving up your arms and causing a sudden swing. Both Tom Watson and David Leadbetter recommend counting to two during the swing. One for the backswing and two for the follow-through.

Finally, without moving, try to listen for the ball to fall in the hole. Many players lift their head up and move their body away from the ball-to-target line at the moment the putter is hitting the ball. This nearly always causes the ball to miss the hole and arc to the left side.

To summarize: aim the putter head first, take up the correct grip (ensuring the grip pressure is light), make sure that your left eye is over the ball at address, and make a pendulum-type swing with good tempo. Then – don't move – listen for the ball to drop into the hole.

Professional Tips

- Off the Tee
- Shots to the Green
- Short Game

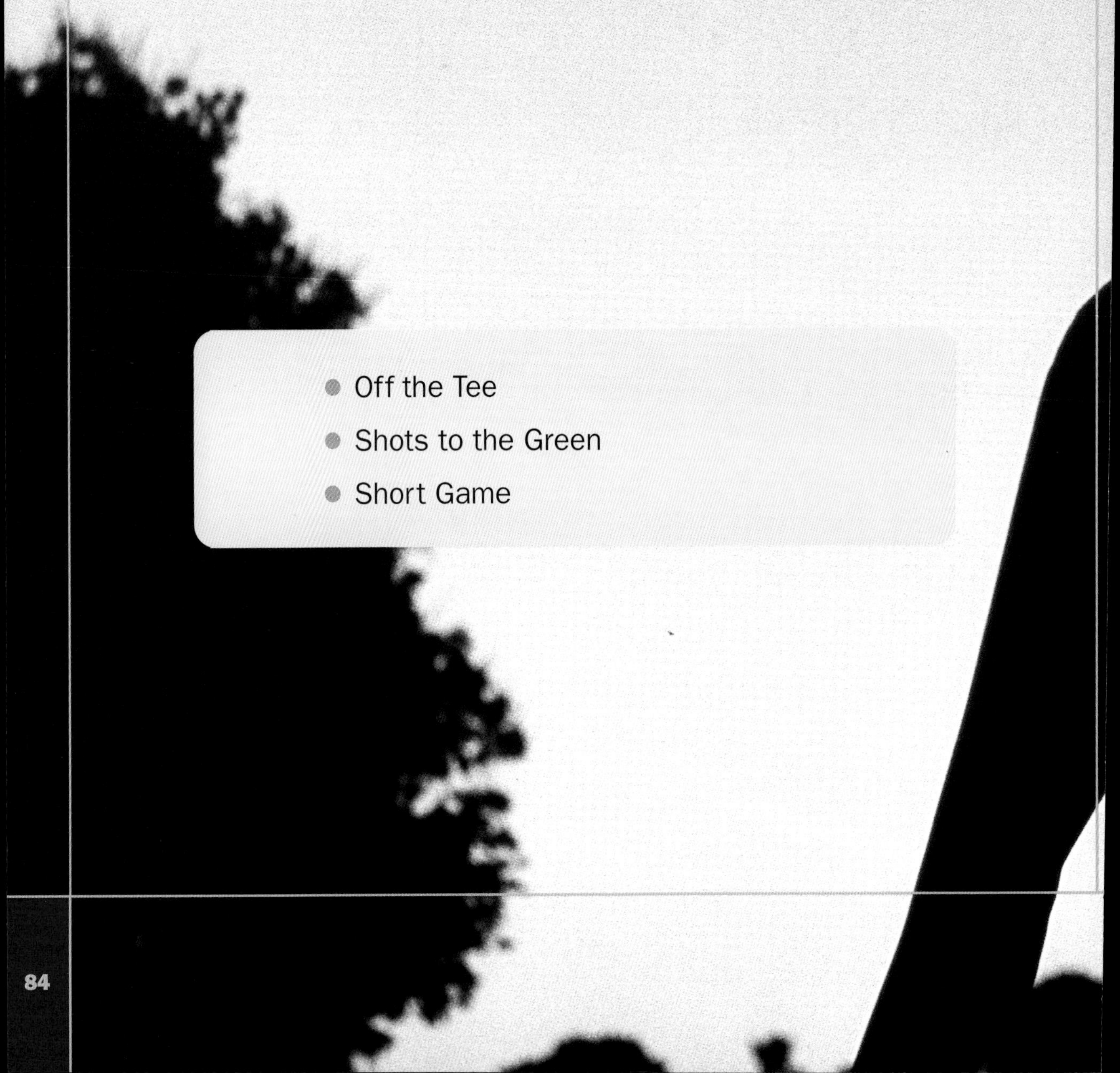

CHAPTER FIVE

Off the Tee

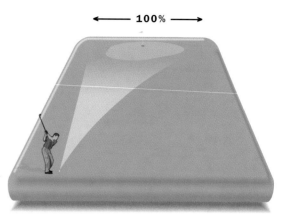

After an initial look at the best ways to warm up before heading out onto the course, this chapter concentrates on the one aspect of the game that seems to fascinate all amateur golfers, and quite a few professionals too: teeing off.

People have always seemed to be totally absorbed with the thought of power and distance so I suppose it should not be a surprise that this should be true in golf. I bet every golfer you know seems to be looking for the ultimate answer to length, accuracy and most importantly consistency off the tee.

Some people believe that the answer lies only in changing one's equipment, and let's face it, we have all been tempted by the brand new incredibly expensive super-duper aerodynamic driver just on the market. And true, a change of equipment may help but if your method is wrong then you will have wasted a lot of money.

The following chapter offers many professional tips that will help improve your technique and thus save you the unnecessary expense of a new driver.

I would like to thank my colleagues for their help in gathering together all the tips in this section of the book. In particular, Danny French, David Mills, Mike Barton, Phil Lewin, and Brad Hauer.

WARMING UP

Before you start hitting any balls, it is advisable to stretch the muscles you are going to use. This will help to minimize the chances of injury and avoid wasting shots on both the range and the course. These exercises will stretch your muscles and help you find your tempo and rhythm before the game.

1 Place a club behind your back and hook your elbows over the clubshaft.

2 Make full swings with your body, ensuring that you make a full shoulder turn.

3 Allow your feet and legs to move as they would if you were hitting balls.

4 Now put the club in your hands but lower it behind you until it is opposite your lower back. Keeping your hands as far apart as possible, raise the club up while keeping your arms straight.

5 Add a few turns of the shoulders; you will feel your upper body, especially the upper back and shoulders, stretching.

6 Keep your feet still to stretch your calves and thighs but don't force your muscles or stretch them too violently.

START SWINGING

I would always recommend working through these routines because, obviously, they help golfers to warm up and stretch their golfing muscles. They also give them an indication of how they are striking the ball that day and if they are going to have to make any allowances on the course. When I say allowances, I mean two things. One is that if for some reason they are not striking the ball particularly well on the range then their strategy on the course will not be overly aggressive. Secondly, if they are hitting the ball on the range with a particular ball flight, such as consistent draw or fade, and if it cannot be immediately rectified on the range they will play the round making allowances for the shape they are hitting. Then they can return to the range after the round to sort out the problem without it having ruined their game.

▶ Hold two short irons in a two-handed baseball grip. Then start making three-quarter swings building up to full swings.

Finish up by making a few practice swings with a single club while concentrating on your turning and rhythm.

▶ You are now ready to hit some golf balls. If you only have 30 minutes to warm up, I suggest the following sequence:

Short Irons	5 minutes
Medium Irons	5 minutes
Long Irons & Woods	5 minutes
Medium Irons	2 to 3 minutes
Short Irons	2 to 3 minutes
Putting	10 minutes

▶ Always start with short-iron shots first, i.e. the pitching wedge or 9-iron. These clubs help you find your rhythm and also encourage you to keep your swing fairly short. Hit balls for approximately 5 minutes. Then move on to the medium irons – 5-, 6-, or 7-irons. Aim at a specific target and place two clubs on the ground to help you with your alignment.

After hitting balls for a further 5 minutes, move on to the long irons and build up to the 5- and 3-woods, finishing with a couple of shots with the driver. Complete this sequence by slowing down with the medium and then short irons, culminating in a few pitch shots.

The last 10 minutes of your warm-up should be spent on the putting green.

Try to find a hole with a relatively flat piece of green in front of it. Taking three balls, practice 2-foot putts, then 4-foot putts, and finish with some 6- and 8-footers. This will give you the confidence to hole out. Now try some 8- and 10-foot putts with some break (borrow) to them. Next, try some downhill and then uphill putts followed by some long putts. This will help you find some touch and feel on the greens. Finish your putting with a few straight 5-footers.

You are now ready to tackle the course.

OFF THE TEE

Many weekend golfers find it hard to hit wood shots because they make the mistake of addressing the ball as they would for an iron shot. In other words, the ball is too far back in the stance and there's too much weight on the left foot at address. With such a long-shafted clubs, this address position will encourage a steep backswing and even promote a reverse pivot. The result of this poor address position is inconsistency with the woods. One minute you will be skying the ball and the next minute you could be topping or hooking or slicing it.

Try to develop a low, sweeping kind of action when playing a wood shot. To do this you should widen your stance a little and position the ball opposite the left heel. Two-thirds of your body weight should be on your right foot at address. Tee up the ball so that the top half of the ball is above the clubhead. This encourages you to hit the ball slightly on the up.

If you have a tendency to snatch the clubhead away at the start of the swing, do not ground the club at address; let it hover above the ground and behind the ball. This will encourage a much smoother, shallower take-away.

How many times have you stood tense and nervous on the first tee? You seem more worried about what other people think of you than concentrating on the task at hand.

Players of all levels suffer from first-tee nerves to some degree. It is good to be nervous, it shows that you care!

SHAPING YOUR TEE SHOT

When you need to shape your tee shot when using the driver, vary the height of your tee. Tee the ball down and your swing will be a little more upright, encouraging cut spin, and the ball will fade (fly out to the right). Tee the ball up higher than normal and the swingpath will flatten, encouraging draw spin and the ball will fly from right to left.

BE POSITIVE

Always be in a positive frame of mind when you stand on the tee with your driver. Many golfers make the mistake of thinking negatively when looking down the fairway, seeing trouble on one side or the other. For example, if you have out-of-bounds down the right-hand side of the fairway, it is natural to start thinking "Do not hit this ball right!" With such a negative thought flowing through your mind you are bound to tense up and fail to make a nice rhythmic swing. Chances are you will slice your tee shot out of bounds. Be positive: instead of thinking about what you must not do, take time to pick out a particular spot at or near your driver range and go for it.

FIRST TEE NERVES

To overcome first-tee nerves and help improve all of your tee shots, try the following: control your breathing, taking long deep breaths and relaxing your body. Tensing your muscles will only affect the rhythm of your swing and prevent you from releasing the club properly at impact. Before you address the ball, stand behind it and visualize the shot you are about to take. When you do stand over the ball, concentrate on where you want the ball to land, not where it could go, such as into trees and bunkers. Finally, think only about tempo as you swing the club. It often helps to visualize swinging a 7-iron rather than a driver.

▼ PRO-WATCHING ▼

No matter what the pressure of being watched by thousands of fans, professionals like Nick Faldo practice complete concentration and focus on the tee.

▶ WHERE ARE YOU GOING?

When driving, always focus on the point on the fairway where you want the ball to land. It sounds obvious but too few golfers appreciate that the tee shot on par-4 and par-5 holes is concerned not primarily with distance but with positioning the ball to make your next shot easier. If you don't aim at a specific target, the ball can go anywhere.

▶ HIT ON THE UP

When driving the ball you should always try to make a low sweeping kind of swing where the clubhead hits the ball after it has passed the lowest point on the swing and is beginning to rise.

A tip I like to use is to ask the player to try to hit the ball clean off the tee without the tee coming out of the ground. I emphasize this by asking him to imagine that the ball is balanced on an upside-down ice-cream cone and he must try not to smash the cone. Both these thoughts can help you make a clean strike on the upside of your swing.

Tony Jacklin used to visualize a green on the fairway exactly where he wanted the ball to land and aim for that rather than the real green.

DON'T GET AHEAD OF YOURSELF

A lot of golfers make the mistake of always trying to keep their hands ahead of the ball at address. Now this philosophy may be correct when playing iron shots, but it most definitely does not apply to wood shots.

With your iron shots, it is imperative that you hit down on the ball first and then take a divot. This is caused by a slower, more upright swing, which in turn is dictated by the length of the clubshaft and the positioning of the clubhead, which is set farther back in the stance than for wood shots. With the

ball positioned farther back in the stance for irons, the hands naturally appear to be ahead of the ball at address. But if you keep the hands in front of the ball when addressing a wood shot, chances are you will hit high, weak shots out to the right.

A wood shot requires a longer, flatter swing and this can be achieved only by pushing the ball farther forward in your stance so that your hands are in line with the clubhead. In the case of the driver, the hands should appear to be slightly behind the ball at address. This will encourage you to hit the ball on the up.

▶ HIT IT HIGH TO HIT IT FURTHER

If you are playing a hole that is downwind, you would be better advised to use a 3-wood than a driver from the tee. The reason is that the 3-wood shot will climb quicker and higher than a driver shot and will carry farther.

Being downwind also means that the ball will have very little backspin, so it will roll farther after impact. Anyway, hitting a 3-wood is easier than hitting a driver any day!

▶ WATCH THE BALL FLY

Many amateurs never realize their true potential off the tee because they are so fixated with keeping their head down. This not only restricts the clearing action of the right shoulder and lower body, but also "freezes" the muscles needed to make a powerful hit through the ball.

I tell my pupils to allow their head to turn, or rotate, out of the shot on the follow-through – almost as if they were trying to watch the ball leave the clubface and fly through the air. But please remember that I said turn the head, not lift it!

TIP

I often see players placing a club across their shoulders just under the chin to check their shoulder alignment. I don't think this particular drill is easy to use. The one I prefer is this: Place a club on the ground in front of your toes and parallel to the ball-to-target line. Next, take two iron clubs and hold them gently against your shoulder blades so that they hang loosely. Now take up your stand and, by looking down each clubshaft, check that they are pointing straight down at the club on the ground. Then draw an imaginary line between the bottom ends of the two clubshafts. This line should be parallel to the club on the ground and to the ball-to-target line.

COURSE MANAGEMENT

Professional golfers always use the teeing ground to their advantage. By this I mean that if they need to hit the ball down the left half of the fairway then they will automatically tee up the ball on the right side of the tee. Alternatively, if they need to hit the ball down the right side of the fairway, they tee up the ball on the left-hand side of the tee. This way they are using all of the fairway to land in.

Play the course, don't let it play you. You can use this philosophy to help with your own game. Over 80% of amateur golfers cut the ball left to right when using a wood. If you tee up the ball on the right side of the tee and aim down the left side of the fairway, you will be using 100% of the available target. If you hit your normal cut, you will finish in the middle of the fairway. Hit a big slice and chances are that, at worst, you will be on the right side of the fairway. If you should hit the ball straight you will probably finish on the left side of the fairway. Of course if you normally hit the ball right to left then the opposite side of the teeing ground applies.

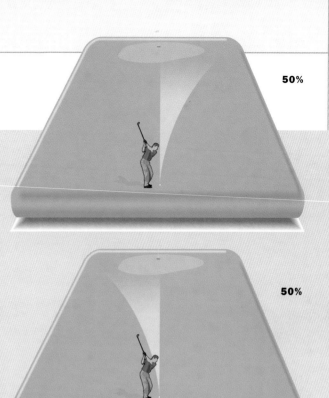

50%

50%

100%

100%

YARDAGE FOR SENIOR GOLFERS

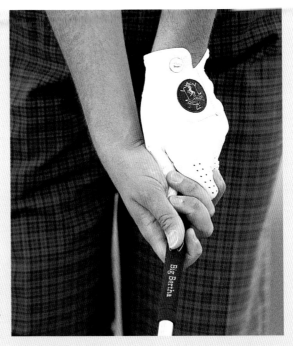

Senior golfers find that the most frustrating thing about advancing years is the distance they lose, especially off the tee. Here are some pointers that will help you regain some of that lost yardage.

Many senior golfers find they lose a lot of flexibility as they get older and that daily stretching exercises help. Concentrate on those that help you turn your shoulders better. This will improve your backswing and your downswing, which is only as good as its backswing.

On the tee, address the ball with your stance a little narrower and with both feet slightly splayed out. Your left arm should be bent a little at the elbow. This combined with allowing your left heel to come up off the ground on the backswing, will lengthen your swing.

Finally hold the club with a hooker's grip (both hands turned slightly more clockwise around the shaft when viewed from the address position) and stand with your feet and hips aiming slightly right of the ball-to-target line but with the clubface square to that line. This encourages a right-to-left ball flight, or draw, which makes the ball run farther when it lands.

Another good tip is to keep in mind that the maximum point of acceleration of the clubhead on the downswing is actually just after you hit the ball. You can take advantage of this by placing the ball farther forward in your stance until it is opposite your left toes. Tee up the ball so that nearly all of it is showing above the clubhead (this is because you will be hitting the ball on the upswing). Now concentrate on where the ball would normally be, say 2 to 3 in (5 to 7 cm) before the new ball position. Do not look at the ball itself! Look at the old ball position. Relax and make your normal swing. You will be amazed at how much farther and straighter you will drive the ball.

▼ PRO-WATCHING ▼

The great golfing legend Ben Hogan used to refer to this as the semi-sitting position. It used to help him to retain yardage on his shots as he got older.

FAIRWAY WOODS

▶ **IMPROVE YOUR STRIKING**

Hitting fairway woods requires a low and smooth sweeping action. If you are struggling with your fairway woods try this simple practice drill.

Using a 3-, 4-, or 5-wood, practice hitting balls on an uphill slope, so that the ball is just above the level of your feet. This will force you to shallow the angle of your swingpath and encourage a low, sweeping angle of attack.

▶ **SLOW DOWN!**

Many golfers, when using a wood or long iron, make a quick backswing in the mistaken belief that the speed will make them hit the ball farther.

When you watch a good player using a wood or long iron you will notice that there is never a rush to take the club away from the ball. A fast backswing destroys rhythm and balance.

Here are two tips to help you produce a consistently smooth movement with those longer clubs.

When you are at your address position, remind yourself that you won't be hitting the ball on the backswing – so don't rush to get back. Sounds obvious, doesn't it? But if used consistently, this mental reminder will, over a period of time, slow you

down. And that allows you more time to get yourself in the right position at the top of the backswing.

This follows from tip number one and gives you a practical picture to help you with that all-important backswing.

Imagine you have a bow and arrow, and just as an archer pulls back slowly and deliberately, so you should adopt the same attitude – pull back slowly and LET GO!

All the hard work is done on the backswing. But, having completed the first half of the swing slowly and smoothly, begin the downswing in the same tempo, accelerating smoothly rather than trying to hit the cover off the ball. Remember, rhythm and tempo get you everywhere in golf.

CHAPTER SIX

Shots to the Green

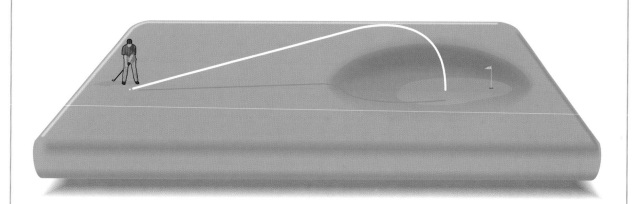

A great many golfers fail to capitalize on a good tee shot due purely to lack of knowledge and experience. It is all very well hitting hundreds of practice balls out on the range and off a nice flat lie but what happens when you have hit a perfectly good tee shot only to find that with your next shot the ball is lying on an upslope? Or how do you compensate for a poor tee shot with your ball in the rough or on the wrong side of the fairway?

If this sounds familiar then read on and learn how to play better and more consistent shots to the green from a range of tips and advice from some of my fellow professionals.

FAIRWAY AND ROUGH SHOTS

The following four tips apply mainly to iron shots, but if the lie of the ball is not too extreme then a fairway wood can be used.

 UPHILL LIE

When playing uphill shots it is important to remember that the ball will fly high and fly to the left, so allowances must be made when setting up. Start by choosing a less-lofted club. The clubface is aimed to the right, as leg movement will be restricted, and the hands will over-compensate when squaring up the clubface at impact. The steeper the slope, the more leg movement is impeded and, consequently, the ball moves even more right-to-left in the air.

1 Position the ball a little farther forward in the stance than normal and try to get your shoulders parallel to the slope.
2 This puts more weight on your lower leg, and to compensate for this, every effort should be made to get the body weight forward in the downswing. Next align the body so it too is aiming to the right of target but is square to the clubface.
3 Finally, concentrate on a nice rhythmic swing, as it is very easy to hit this type of shot too hard.

1   **2**   **3**

▶ DOWNHILL LIE

The downhill lie is played "opposite" to how an uphill lie is played. The downhill slope will de-loft the club and hit the ball lower. Because the backswing is fairly upright, chances are the ball will move from left to right in flight, so allowances for this must be made at address.

1   The clubface is aimed to the left to allow for the cut spin, and the ball is positioned farther back in the stance to make for better contact with the steeper backswing.

2   As with the uphill shot, your shoulders should be parallel to the slope and the weight once again favoring the lower leg.

3   At the moment of impact, try to stay down on the ball and allow the club to "chase" down the slope.

▶ BALL ABOVE FEET

When the ball is above your feet at address, the swingpath will flatten and this in turn encourages a right-to-left flight pattern (hookspin).

Obviously, the clubface and body lines must aim to the right of target to compensate for the hookspin. Your hands will need to go down the shaft and the ball should be positioned toward the center of your stance. Try to keep your body weight toward your toes to compensate for the tendency, when swinging, to fall back away from the ball.

▶ BALL BELOW FEET

With the ball below the feet, there is a tendency to hit the ball from left to right (cutspin) because you are forced to adopt a very upright swing. Once again, the clubface and body lines must compensate for this by aiming to the left of target. You will appear to be standing closer to the ball than usual, but in fact you are really standing farther away, so hold the club as far up the grip as you can to extend your swing. Flex the knees more than usual and try to keep your weight on your heels, as there is a tendency to topple toward the ball during the downswing. Try to maintain the same amount of knee flex during the swing as at address as there is a tendency to lose height on the backswing – don't "sit" farther down. Try to keep a steady rhythm – as always – throughout the shot.

▶ PLAYING INTO THE WIND (PUNCH SHOT)

Many amateur golfers struggle when playing shots into the wind. One of Tom Watson's favorite sayings is, "Swing with ease, into the breeze," but of course this can only be done with correct technique.

The shot that you need to practice for playing into the wind is called the punch shot, although I think the name encourages people to hit the ball too hard, putting too much backspin on the ball and if anything making the ball fly even higher than normal. I much prefer to use the term "knock-down shot," which in essence is what the shot is.

A common mistake is when the player positions the ball too far back in the stance, almost opposite the right foot! This only encourages the golfer to lift the club up more with hands and arms, and the shot is either smothered or blocked out to the right.

1 I like to see the ball positioned just back (or right) of center of your stance. The most club you should use is a 4- or 5-iron, bearing in mind that, because you have pushed the ball back in your stance, you have in effect de-lofted the club.

Next, choke down a little on the grip. This gives you a bit more fuel and helps to shorten your swing. About two-thirds of your body weight should favor your left side at address – and should stay there throughout the swing.
2 Now make a comfortable three-quarter backswing.
3 Concentrate on a restricted three-quarter follow-through.

I like to encourage my pupils to keep their hands "soft" throughout the swing, thereby reducing the impulse to hit the ball too hard.

SHAPING THE BALL

When playing a round of golf there will be occasions when you will need to shape your shots – that is, to hit a fade (when the ball moves slightly from left to right) or a draw (the ball moves right to left). There will even be times when you will need to hit a deliberate hook or slice.

▶ THE DRAW

In the draw shot, the ball moves from right to left just as it nears the apex of its flight. To hit a draw, set your ball-to-target line and parallel body lines (shoulder, hips, and feet) so that they are aiming right of target (where you want the ball to start). Next, turn the club in your grip so that the clubface is aiming at the end target (where you want the ball to finish). Concentrate on an imaginary target that is on line with where you want the ball to

start, otherwise it is very easy to pull the club toward the end target, which results in a pull hook. Lighten your grip to assist in a full release of the clubhead at impact.

If you should need to hit a big hook, set up as you would for a draw but use a stronger grip, with both hands turned slightly farther clockwise around the shaft. Also remember to use a more lofted club as the ball will fly lower and run farther on landing.

▶ THE FADE

With the fade, the ball moves from left to right when it reaches the apex of its flight.

The opposite rules apply to a fade, as compared with a draw. The clubface should still aim toward where you want the ball to finish, but the ball-to-target line and parallel body line (feet, hips, and shoulders) should aim at an imaginary target that is to the left of where you want your shot to finish.

When playing a fade, hold your hands a little higher at address and hold the club a little tighter with the last three fingers of the left hand. This prevents you from closing the clubface at impact and thus hitting the ball straight left. If you should need to slice the ball, remember to have a weaker grip, positioning the hands more on top of the shaft. Remember to use less lofted club, as the ball will fly higher and not travel as far as a draw.

When playing from a good lie in the rough, golfers are often surprised by how the ball responds when they hit it. Sometimes it flies low and long, and sometimes it flies high and short. The reason for this inconsistency comes down to the way the grass is growing. If the grass is leaning toward the target (see above) you get a flier, which comes out of the rough on a low trajectory, landing with very little backspin, and thus running farther than normal. To counter this effect, use a more lofted club and aim to land the ball short of the target.

If the grass is growing away from the target (see above), the ball travels a much shorter distance than normal because the grass around the ball tends to wrap around the clubhead, reducing its momentum.

You may also find that grass snatches at the hosel, which in turn closes the clubface. This leads to a smothered shot that flies left. The answer is to use a more lofted club and to grip the club a little tighter to prevent the clubface from closing. With this type of lie in heavy rough, it is best to be realistic and play the percentage shot: play-out sideways to the nearest part of the fairway. You may drop a shot – but you risk dropping more than one if you are too bold.

PLAY SAFE FROM THE ROUGH

Always look to play the percentage shot. Too many golfers get overly ambitious. The only time you can afford to get aggressive in the rough is when the ball is sitting up in the semi, or first cut of, rough. Anything worse and you will have to "play out." In that case decide where you would ideally like to play your next shot, and which club you will need to get the ball there.

One problem you face when playing from deep rough is grass that will get trapped between the ball and clubface at impact. The other is the grass beyond the ball. In the shot, long grass grabs hold of the neck of the club and hooks the face. After impact, yet more grass cushions the blow, leading to a smothered shot.

Stand to the ball with a fairly open stance and an open clubface. Locate the ball a little farther forward in your stance than normal and allow the club to hover rather than grounding it. Hold the club tighter than usual – but not excessively – and make a positive, aggressive swing but with a reasonable length of follow-through.

If the ball is lying very badly in long rough, cut your losses and play out sideways. Locate the ball farther back in your stance and leave the clubface open. Play the shot as if it were a plugged bunker shot by making a very steep upright backswing and a short follow-through.

GET YOUR WEIGHT RIGHT

Few golfers realize how important weight distribution at address really is. It helps to determine the steepness of the swing and therefore the trajectory of the shot. For fairway woods and long irons, about two-thirds of your body weight should favor your right side. This encourages a low, wide backswing and a sweeping action through the ball. Medium-iron shots should see your weight evenly distributed, while your short-iron shots should be played with about two-thirds of your weight favoring the left side to encourage a descending blow.

Right: Tom Watson is famed for his skill in getting out of the rough.

PLAYING A SHOT OUT OF AN OLD DIVOT

Set Up

Finish

▶ Possibly one of the most frustrating experiences on a golf course is when you have hit a perfectly good drive, only to find your ball sitting in an old divot mark. With the right technique, however, you can limit the damage caused by this piece of bad luck.

The goal is to hit down and through the divot, and to do this the golfer must make some alterations to his conventional stance. To encourage

you to hit down on the downswing, the ball must be positioned farther back in the stance than normal and your body weight should favor the left side.

Grip down the shaft a little to encourage a wristy three-quarter swing, and use a more lofted club than normal, as your ball position will deloft the clubface.

Make a controlled swing and try to feel that you are driving downward at impact.

FAIRWAY BUNKER SHOTS

The fairway bunker shot is without doubt the hardest shot in golf. It is a difficult enough shot for professionals who have a sound technique, but for a weekend golfer it can be a nightmare. However, by using these exercises you will soon see a vast improvement in your shots.

First things first: pick a club that you know will send the ball comfortably clear of the front lip of the bunker. Next, take your stance with the ball set farther back in your stance than normal. This helps ensure that you hit the ball first and the sand second. Now wiggle your feet down a little into the sand. This gives your swing a firm base and also helps "quiet" your legs throughout the swing. Grip down the club by 1 to 2 in (5 to 7 cm) to shorten your swing and encourage a quieter turn through the ball.

I like to see a player keep his chin up off his chest, and I ask my pupils to imagine they are standing on a sheet of ice. This encourages them to make a quiet swing of even tempo, which results in a clean strike.

OTHER FAIRWAY PROBLEMS

▶ WHY GO ROUND WHEN YOU CAN GO OVER?

How many times have you been stuck behind an obstacle like a tree and have failed to fly the ball over it? Quite a few times I should think. Many golfers think that the answer is to use a lofted club and just belt the ball hard. But 9 times out of 10 this fails to deliver. With the correct technique, however, you can be successful 9 times in 10 attempts.

First of all, place the ball farther forward in your stance and allow two-thirds of your body weight to favor the right side at address. This encourages your hands to be over the ball instead of in front of it, which puts a little more loft on the club.

The clubface should be aiming at the target but your feet, hips, and shoulders should be aiming slightly left of target. This puts cutspin on the ball, making it fly higher. Make a comfortable swing and concentrate on "staying behind the ball" through impact, and completing a high finish.

▶ FLIERS

You may well have heard the expression "fliers" used by golf commentators on television about a ball that flies much farther than the player intended. Fliers are quite common when playing out of a fluffy lie in the rough, especially in wet conditions. A flier occurs when grass or water gets trapped between the back of the ball and the clubface at impact. The result is a low-flying shot with little or no backspin, so that the ball rolls farther than usual on landing. Adjustments should be made to allow for this: either use a more lofted club or try to hit a fade, which creates a little more backspin.

▶ PLAYING THE PERCENTAGES

When playing a long approach shot into a green, devote a moment or two to considering where would be the best place to miss the green. Sounds silly doesn't it? – but few amateur golfers pay serious attention to where the trouble is around the green. If there are bunkers and hazards at the front of the green then take out at least one more club. If the trouble is at the back of the green then take one less club. Too many golfers, when selecting a club, think only of their best shot, not their average shot.

▶ PERCHED LIE

Golfers often struggle with clubbing when hitting a ball that is "perched" up in the rough. Most will try to hit a normal shot, which results in the ball being hit with the top half of the clubhead and the ball just pops up in the air and does not travel the full distance intended.

Ideally one should try to "pick" the ball off the top of the rough, and this can be done by gripping down the handle of the club and allowing the clubhead to hover just above the grass. Now make a swing but imagine that the ball is sitting on a tee. This will help prevent you from hitting down the shot and "popping' the ball up.

▶ PLAYING TO A TARGET ABOVE AND BELOW

Always remember that when you play into a green that is above you, the ball will land "hot" and will have little backspin. Conversely when you play into a green below you, the ball will land softly.

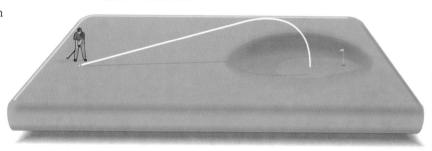

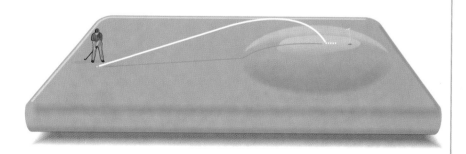

CHAPTER SEVEN

Short Game

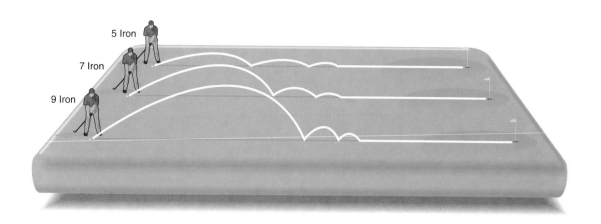

5 Iron

7 Iron

9 Iron

As I promised earlier in the book, in the following chapter you will find many useful tips for your short game.

The short game or scoring zone to some professionals is often the difference between a poor golfer and a good one. There is little point in hitting the ball miles off the tee and playing arrow-straight second and third shots into greens if at the end of it all you still cannot get the ball into the hole.

Some of the world's greatest golfers can be, professionally speaking, very wayward sometimes but more than compensate for it by having exquisite short games. Prime examples include Seve Ballesteros, Ben Crenshaw, Jose Maria-Olazabal, and even the legendary Tom Watson in his prime. As the old saying goes, "You drive for show, and putt for dough."

CHIPPING

Many players who have trouble chipping, may be hitting the ground before the ball, which causes either a fat shot or a thin shot.

The following is an excellent practice-ground drill to help develop a more positive strike into the back of the ball. Place a small coin in front of the ball and load your weight more onto your left side, with the ball position in line with your right heel. Now start hitting some shots, trying to strike both the ball and the coin.

You will find that you are now playing your chip shots with a slightly descending blow and that your hands are naturally ahead of the ball at impact.

TIP

Always bear in mind that it takes a better than average chip to match an average putt. Chip or pitch a ball only when you cannot use a putter.

THE "PUTT CHIP"

If the ball is close to the green, the simplest and safest way to chip is to use the "putt chip." The idea behind the putt chip is to play the stroke almost as you would for a putt. This removes any wrist action from the shot and leads to greater consistency.

1 Using an 8- or 9-iron, assume your normal putting grip and stance, but position the ball farther back in your stance than normal. You must ensure that your hands are slightly ahead of the ball at address and that your weight favors your left side.

2 and 3 You will notice that, because you are standing closer to the ball than normal for a chip shot, the heel of the club is slightly off the ground. This is fine as you should hit the ball with the "dead" part of the club, the toe. Keeping your elbows splayed, use your normal, smoothly accelerating putting stroke. If you need to hit the ball farther, just make a longer swing.

▶ CHIPPING FROM HARDPAN

If you have to play a chip shot from "hardpan" (hard bare ground) it is important to exaggerate the changes in address that you adopt for normal chipping. The ball should be pushed even farther back in your stance, and even more weight should be placed on your left side. This ensures that you hit the ball first and the ground second. Otherwise the club will bounce, resulting in a thinned low, running shot.

Above all, never use a sand iron for this shot; a sand iron's big rounded sole is designed to bounce the clubhead up off the ground. Use a pitching wedge or 9-iron, and make sure that your hands stay ahead of the clubhead through impact.

Bellied Wedge

Wood Shot

▶ CHIPPING AGAINST THE FRINGE

It is always frustrating when you hit what appears to be a good approach shot at the pin, only to find that the ball has rolled through the green and has finished up tight against the fringe of the rough surrounding the green. It's too difficult a shot to chip and virtually impossible to putt – so how should it be played?

There are two possible choices: One is a "bellied" sand wedge; the other is a putt using a wood. The bellied sand wedge is a shot where the intention is to not use the loft of the club. Address the ball as if you were going to putt it. Choke down on the grip, and allow the clubhead to hover above the grass and level with the equator of the ball. Now putt the ball, aiming to catch it on or slightly above its equator with the leading edge of the blade. A bellied sand wedge shot requires a good deal of practice, but it's widely used by professional golfers. If the grass is too high to use a sand wedge, play the same shot using a 4- or 5-wood. Tiger Woods is a master of this shot, playing it with a 3-wood.

PITCHING

1 **2** **3**

▶ THE PITCH AND RUN

To play the pitch and run, you must stand square to the ball-to-target line, with the ball positioned farther back than normal. Your body weight should favor your left side and your grip pressure should be light. The swing should be of even tempo, accelerating smoothly through the ball, as any attempt to "hit" the ball will result in backspin. Finally, concentrate on allowing your forearms to roll over on the follow-through as they would for a normal swing. Do not attempt to hold the clubface open through impact – this creates undesirable backspin. At the finish of the swing, the toe of the club should be pointing skyward.

Many golfers make the mistake of allowing their hands and arms to do all the work and wonder why their pitching is so inconsistent. Always remember that the pitch shot, with a few adjustments, is a scaled-down version of the full swing. And the full swing is properly done with the whole body. To pitch, it is imperative that you use the bigger muscles to control the distance you want to hit the ball.

A good drill to encourage this use of the bigger muscles is the famous towel drill favored by Nick Faldo and David Leadbetter.

1 Simply tuck a towel under your arms and across your chest. Choke down the grip a little and take your normal pitching stance.

2 and **3** Now play some short pitch shots trying to keep the towel in place. If you need to hit the ball a little farther simply turn your chest more quickly.

▶ In all the pitching lessons I give, the problems always seem to occur within 20 yards of the green. At the 20-yard range, two faults commonly occur among medium- to high-handicap golfers.

The first is deceleration of the clubhead on the downswing. Too many golfers, when they get close to the green, get too shy when pitching. It almost appears that the golf ball itself is a barrier and the golfer is reluctant to get the clubhead past it following impact. This negative swing thought encourages the hands and arms to decelerate on the downswing, so that the golfer quits on the shot and moves the ball barely halfway to the target. It is imperative that you accelerate the clubhead through the shot. Be positive and be aggressive.

The second most common fault is that many golfers fail to understand what they are trying to achieve with a pitch shot. They seem to think that by looking at the bottom of the flag then the ball is bound to finish close or even go in, though this is rarely the case.

A good pitcher will concentrate not on the pin but on the point where he wants the ball to land, and he then works out how the ball will run from there, almost as if he were lining up a putt. After he has made some adjustments for how the ball will roll, he forgets about the flag and the hole and concentrates purely on the ball-landing zone.

▶ **FROM THE ROUGH TO THE GREEN**

If your ball is sitting in deep rough, then a few adjustments need to be made to both the set-up and the swing itself.

Your stance should be slightly open (aiming left) in relation to the ball-to-target line and the clubface should be slightly closed (aiming just right).

It is imperative that you avoid getting too much grass trapped between the clubhead and ball at impact. To achieve this you need to swing the club back on a much steeper plane than normal, so place the ball farther back in your stance and put a little more weight on your left side. Do not ground the club, just let it hover above the grass to encourage as clean a strike as possible. Slide your hands down the grip a little and hold the club a little more tightly than normal.

Now make a three-quarter backswing and punch down into the back of the ball. There will be little if any backspin on the ball so it will have plenty of run on it when it hits the green.

BUNKER PLAY

▶ LONG BUNKER SHOTS

One of the most awkward bunker shots a golfer can face during a round of golf is the 40- to 70-yard bunker shot. This is a difficult shot for the seasoned professional, let alone a weekend golfer.

Address the ball with the clubface square to the target and the ball positioned toward the center of your stance. The body line (shoulders, hips, feet) should run slightly left (or open) of target as this encourages a three-quarter-length swing. Grip down the shaft a little and try to keep your weight on your left side throughout the swing. The important things to remember when playing a long bunker shot are to avoid using a sand wedge, and to allow your hands to release at impact. Remember also to take into account that the ball will roll when it hits the green.

▶ PLAYING FROM WET SAND

Too often golfers try to play a normal "explosion" or "splash" style of bunker shot when their ball is sitting on wet sand. This will only encourage the clubhead to bounce too early on the hard, wet sand, resulting in a thinned shot straight into the face of the bunker.

To remedy this you require a much steeper swing that encourages the clubhead to dig into the sand before it bounces out. For this, have the ball a little farther back in the stance and square up the clubface. Instead of aiming 2 or 3 in (5 or 7 cm) behind the ball as you would for a normal bunker shot, allow only half an inch (a centimeter or two) of sand behind the ball. Now make a fairly upright swing with the hands and arms, and hit down and through. If the sand is relatively level and the lip of the bunker is very low, you may well be able to chip the ball out with a pitching wedge or 9-iron. In extreme cases, you might even putt the ball out.

Always test the quality and depth of the sand by wriggling your feet. Wet or coarse sand creates a firm base that increases the bounce of the club, therefore the clubface should be square at address. If the sand is fluffy, fine, and dry, the club will dig in more, so open the clubface more to increase the bounce.

One of my favorite tips for playing an explosion shot is designed to stop you from closing the face of the club at impact: Simply imagine that at impact you have a glass of water resting on the clubface that you must not spill on the follow-through.

▶ TEE THE BALL UP

To help you get used to slicing the clubhead through the sand and lifting the ball out on a bed of sand, try this neat little tip next time you practice:

Put your ball on a tee in the bunker and press down until you can no longer see the tee. Now try to play a conventional splash shot but concentrate on digging the tee out of the sand with a long shallow divot. It is also important to concentrate on a long, high finish with the hands and arms.

1   **2**   **3**

▶ TAKING SAND

Amateurs very often find it difficult to take the correct amount of sand when playing bunker shots. If you fall into this category, try this simple practice tip.

1 In a practice bunker, draw a line in the sand 2 to 2½ in (5 to 6 cm) behind the ball.

2 Now try to hit that line with the leading edge of your sand wedge on the downswing.

3 After your shot, check to see how close you were to the line.

Repeat this many times, always remembering to try to "explode" or "splash" the sand out of the bunker and to accelerate the clubhead into a high finish.

When you go onto the course and find yourself in a bunker needing to play an "explosion" shot, focus on a grain of sand 2 to 2½ in (5 to 6 cm) behind the ball and blast the sand on the way to that high finish. Just watch the ball pop out every time.

PUTTING

▶ KEEP ON TRACK

Many golfers struggle to keep the putter head on the ball-to-target line long enough and find they are struggling to hole putts. This can be corrected with this simple drill. Space out five tees on each side of your putter head, on a level part of the green and parallel to your ball-to-target line. Make sure that the gap between the two lines of tees is just wide enough for your putter to pass through.

Now start putting, concentrating on making an even-tempo swing and avoiding contact with the tees. At first you may find this difficult, but you will soon get used to it. The goal is to achieve a consistent putting stroke where the putter head stays on line with the hole for as long as possible.

TIP

Before you go out to play on the course, you should always spend 10 to 15 minutes practicing on the putting green. It is always useful to practice short, medium, and long putts, but I like to finish by hitting 10 or more putts to a target smaller than a golf hole.

Hitting 10-foot putts to a tee stuck in the green does wonders for your tempo. More importantly, it gives you a huge confidence boost for when you get out on the course. After all, if you can hit a tee with a golf ball, imagine how big the holes will look!

Wrong Set-Up   **Correct Set-Up**

▶ PRACTICE FOR FEEL

Try this simple routine when you next play.

Go through your normal pre-shot routine, and address the ball.

Before you hit the ball, turn your eyes down the ball-to-target line until you are looking at the hole. Now, without returning your eyes to the ball, make your stroke. It will take a little getting used to but you will soon find that your feel has improved. One word of caution: make sure that, when you look at the hole, your eyes are parallel to the ball-to-target line. In other words, *turn* – don't lift – your head.

▶ PRACTICE THE REAL THING

Too many players do not take their practice putting strokes seriously enough. How many times have you seen someone take two or three quick practice putting strokes, then stand to the ball and make a complete hash of the real thing. The practice-putting stroke should always be thought of as a full dress-rehearsal for the real thing. After you have thought about all the information you have gathered for the impending putt – slopes, breaks, the speed of the green – you should practice the stroke that will get the ball in the hole. Do not commit yourself to the putt until you are sure you have "programmed" the required speed and line into your practice swing. Only then should you step up to the ball.

| 1 | 2 | 3 |

▶ PUTTING WITH A SAND WEDGE

A useful drill to help you obtain the right putting stroke is to putt with a sand wedge. Grip down the club and hold it as if you were using your putter.

1 Make an even-tempo stroke at the ball while aiming to make contact with the ball's equator or just above.

2 and 3 This encourages you to take back the putter low to the ground and teaches you to strike the ball on the up, both of which enable you to get good roll on your putts.

> **TIP**
>
> When lining up a medium- or long-distance putt, remember the following: Sixty percent of a putt's break will normally occur within 3 feet (1 meter) of the hole. Unless there are exceptional circumstances, any slopes at the beginning of the putt have very little influence on the end result.

INDEX